COMPLETE BLUES GUITAR BOOK

BY MIKE CHRISTIANSEN

Online Audio & Video

Audio
www.melbay.com/94682BCDEB
Video
dv.melbay.com/94682
YouTube
www.melbay.com/94682V

Audio Contents

WWW.MELBAY.COM

To my wife, Kathy, and my children Corey, Dustin, Ashley, and Emily.
I thank them for their encouragement and for allowing me to hide and work on the book.

Introduction

At the root of rock n'roll and jazz is the blues. With its origins in the United States, this style of music has become popular and influenced music the world over. This book presents the necessary elements for playing blues guitar. Many of the techniques shown in this book were used by the earliest blues players such as: Robert Johnson, Lightning Hopkins, Mississippi John Hurt, Bill Broonzy, Lonnie Johnson, and others. These techniques are still popular and are used today. Early blues guitarists used acoustic (non-electric) guitars. Although many of the accompaniment patterns and solos in this book are intended for acoustic guitar, they will sound good on the electric guitar as well.

The Author — Mike Christiansen

Mike Christiansen is an associate professor and Director of Guitar Studies at Utah State University. He has his B.M. and M.M. degrees, is the author of several books, and has written and recorded jingles and music for television. He has also done solo concerts, back-up work on recordings, and played with various bands and ensembles. Mr. Christiansen often serves as a clinician, as well.

Contents

Explanation of Notation

The chords, scales, and arpeggio patterns in this book are shown with diagrams such as the one drawn below. In the diagrams, the vertical lines represent the string with the 1st string being on the right. The horizontal lines represent the frets. The dots show where to place left hand fingers. The numbers on, or next to, the dots show which left hand finger to use. With the chords, the loop under the diagram shows how many strings are to be strummed.

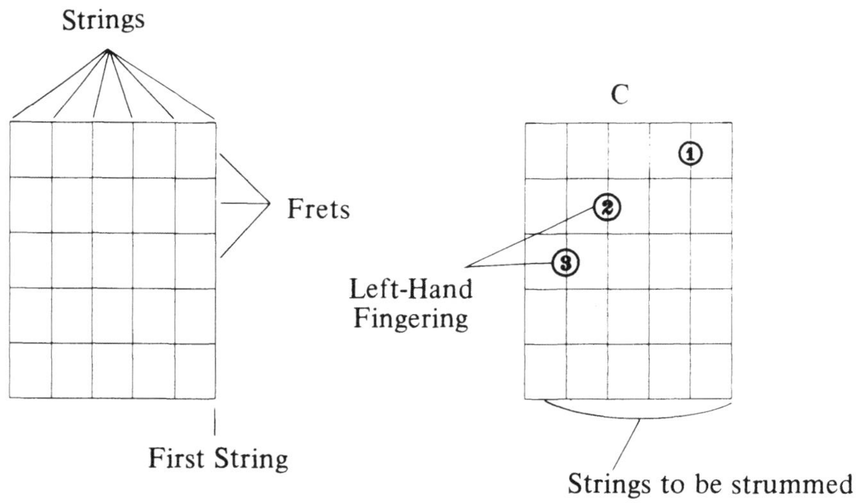

The exercises and solos in this book are written in standard notation and tablature. The numbers under the standard notation indicate left - hand fingering. Circled numbers next to the notes indicate on which string the note is to be played.

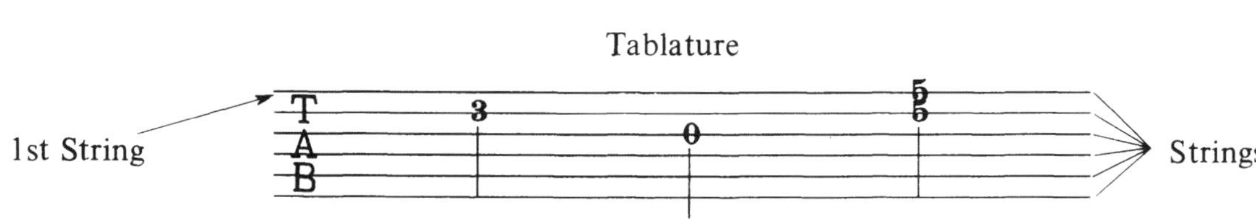

The six horizontal lines in tablature represent the strings. The top line is the first string. A number on the line indicates the fret in which to place a finger.

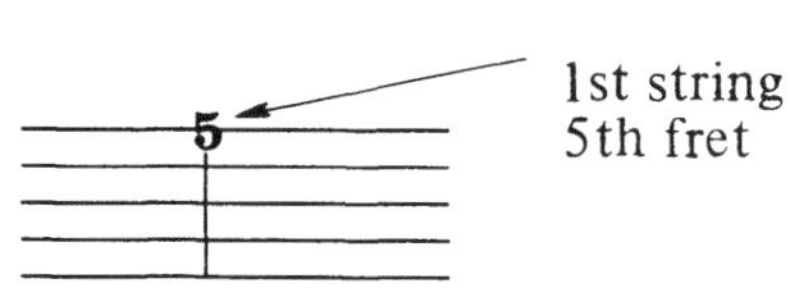

The stems under the numbers indicate the rhythm. One stem under a number means that note would get one beat.

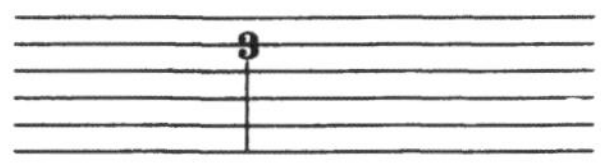

If two or more numbers appear on top of one another, play the strings at the same time.

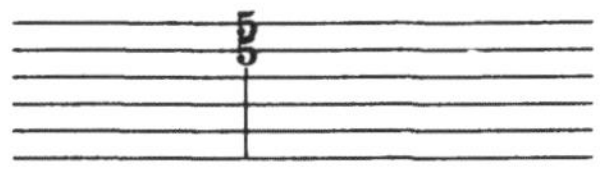

The circled numbers indicate which left-hand finger should be used to push on the string.

Explanation of Special Notation

⊓ Downstroke. This sign above a note indicates to pick the string using a downstroke.

V Upstroke. This sign above a note indicates to pick the string using an upstroke.

Tie: If two of the same notes are connected with a loop, play only the first note and let it ring through the time value of the second note.

Hammer-On: Strike the first note, then sound the second note by pushing down the finger without picking the string again.

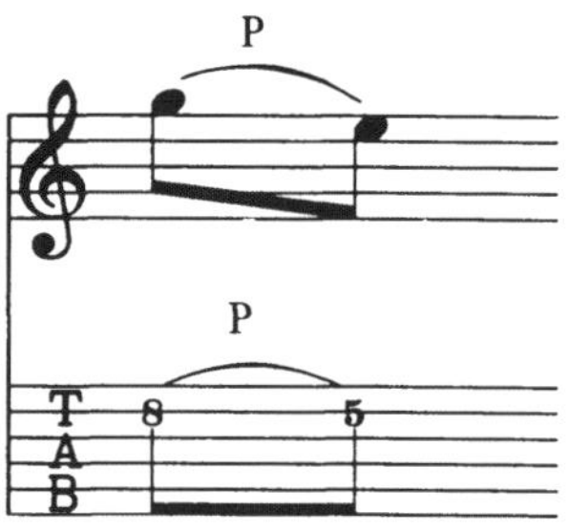

Pull-Off: Strike the first note, then sound the second note by pulling the finger off of the first note. It is important to place both of the fingers down when striking the first note.

Half-Step Bend: Strike the string and then bend it up ½ step.

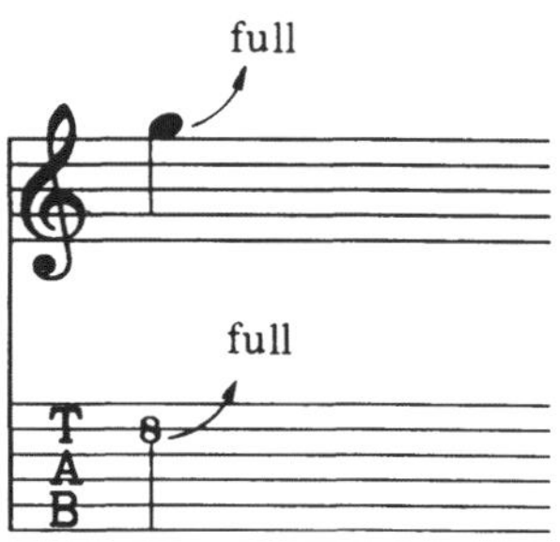

Whole-Step Bend: Strike the string and then bend it up one whole (full) step.

Slide: Strike the first note and then slide the same finger along the string to the second note.

Slide Up: Slide from two frets below up to the indicated note.

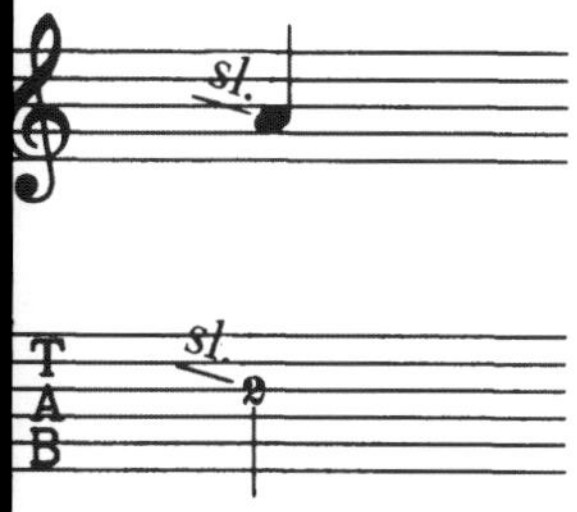

Slide Down: Slide from two frets above down to the written note.

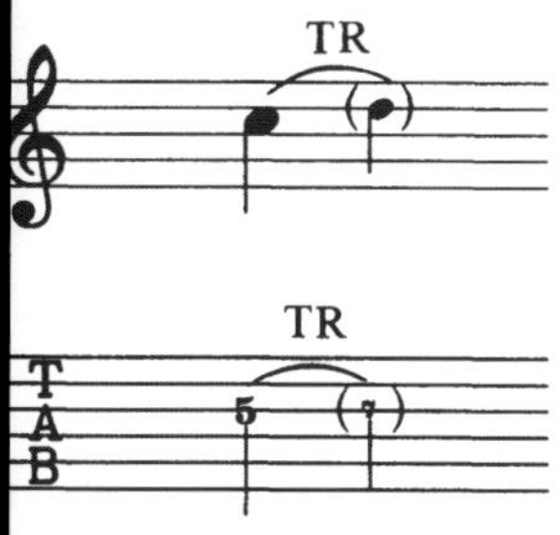

Trill: Play the first written note and then, with a series of hammer-ons and pull-offs, play the note in parentheses.

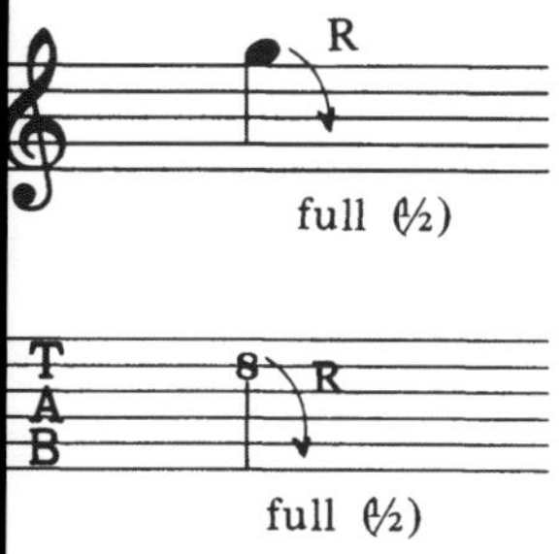

Bend Release: Place a finger on the indicated note and bend the string a full (or half) step. Strike the string and release the bend back to the written note.

Time Values

The following time values apply if the bottom number in the time signature is a 4. If the bottom number in the time signature is an 8 rather than a 4, all of the time values are doubled.

	NAME	TIME VALUE
	Quarter Note	1 beat
	Half Note: Pick the note on the 1st beat and let it sound through the 2nd beat.	2 beats
	Dotted half note: The dot behind the note increases the length of the note by ½ its original value.	3 beats
	Whole Note	4 beats

Eighth Note — ½ beat

Dotted Quarter Note — 1 ½ beats

Sixteenth Note — ¼ beat

Eighth Note Triplet — Three notes to 1 beat

Quarter Note Triplet — Three notes to 2 beats

Quarter Rest — 1 beat

Dotted Quarter Rest 1½ beats

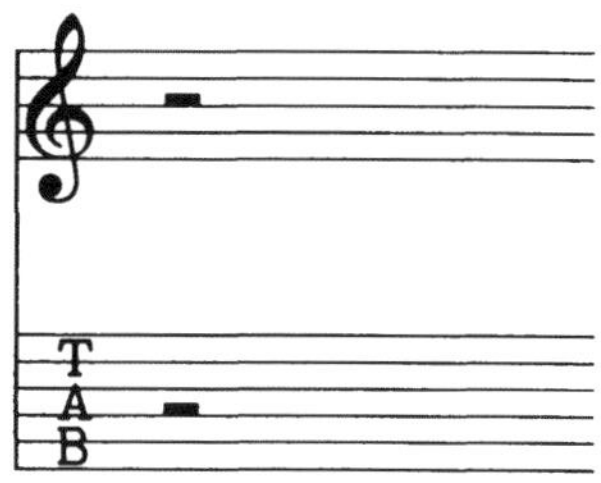

Half rest 2 beats

Dotted Half Rest 3 beats

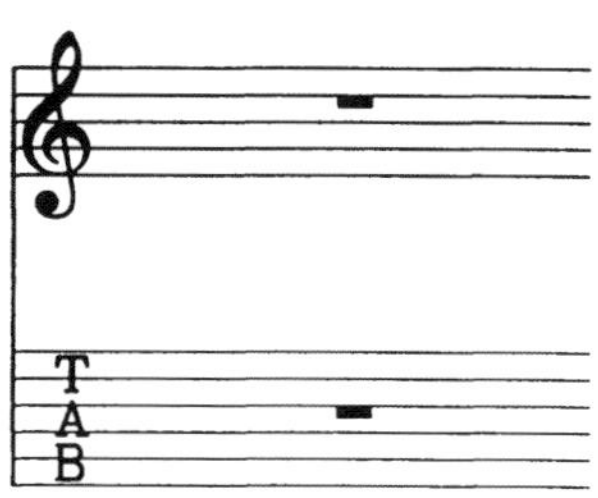

Whole Rest 4 beats

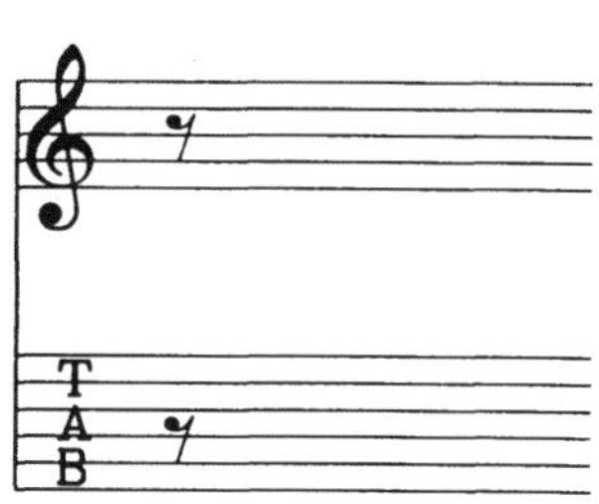

Eighth Rest ½ beat

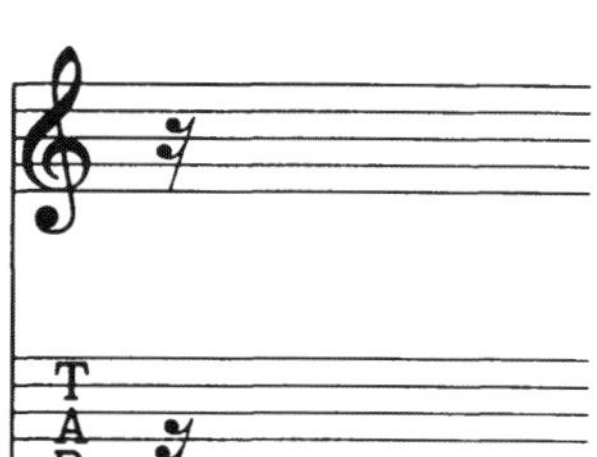

Sixteenth Rest ¼ beat

Strumming Notation

Strum bar: Strum the chord which is written above the strum bar one time. If the bottom number of the time signature is a "4" (4/4, 3/4), the strum gets one beat.

Downstroke: When this sign appears above the strum bar ( ), it means to strum the chord down.

V

Upstroke: When this sign appears above the strum bar ( ), it means to strum the chord up. Play only the first two or three strings with the upstroke.

Half-note strum: This strum gets two beats. Strum the chord on the first beat and let it ring through the second beat.

Dotted half strum: This strum gets three beats. Strum the chord on the first beat and let it ring for two more beats.

Whole-note strum: This strum gets four beats.

Staccato strum: The dot above the strum bar indicates the strum is very short rather than sustained. This is done by quickly releasing the pressure on the strings immediately after the strum. Don't lift the left-hand fingers completely off the strings. This type of strum can also be done by quickly touching the palm of the right hand on the strings after the strum.

>

Accent: When this sign appears above a strum bar ( ), it indicates to play that strum more loudly.

Muted strum: The muted strum is done by touching the palm of the right hand on the strings near the bridge. Do this just before the pick strikes the strings. This creates a muted or "dead" sound. The muted strum can also be done when playing barre chords by releasing the pressure with the left-hand fingers. Still touch the strings, but don't push them down. The following is a strum pattern using the muted strum:

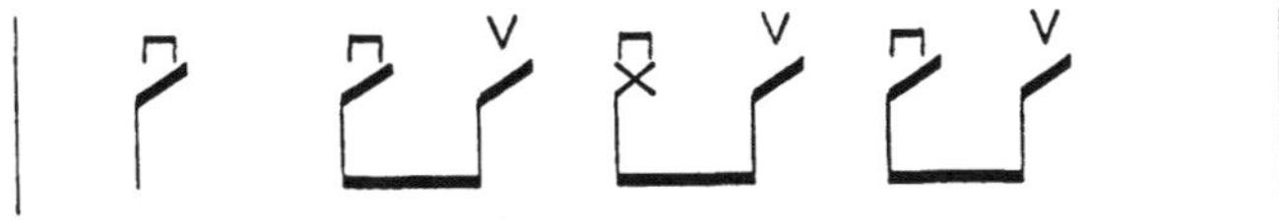

Eighth strum: This strum gets ½ beat if the bottom number of the time signature is a "4." If the bottom number is an "8," this strum would get one beat. It is the equivalent of an eighth note.

If the bottom number of the time signature is a "4," two strum bars connected together with a beam indicate two strums in one beat. The first strum is counted as the number of the beat, and the second strum is counted as "and."

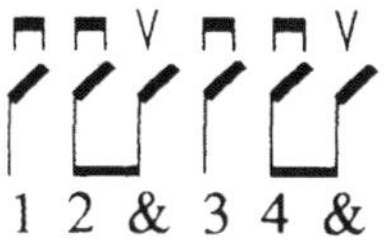

Strum pattern: This would be a strum pattern for 4/4 time. The rhythm (the way in which the pattern is counted) is written below the pattern.

Tie: When the tie connects two strum bars, play the first strum and let it ring through the time value of the second strum.

Triplet strum: Three bars connected with a beam indicates to play three strums to a beat. Triplets should be counted as "one-trip-let, two-trip-let," etc.

1-trip-let

Sixteenth strum: This strum gets ¼ beat if the bottom number of the time signature is a 4. If the bottom number of the time signature is an 8, this strum gets ½ beat.

1 e & a

Four strum bars connected with two beams indicate four strums to one beat. The strums should be counted "one-ee-and-a." It is the equivalent of four sixteenth notes.

Written below are various combinations of eighth and sixteenth notes. Notice the suggested strum directions and how the rhythms are counted. Hold any chord and practice these patterns:

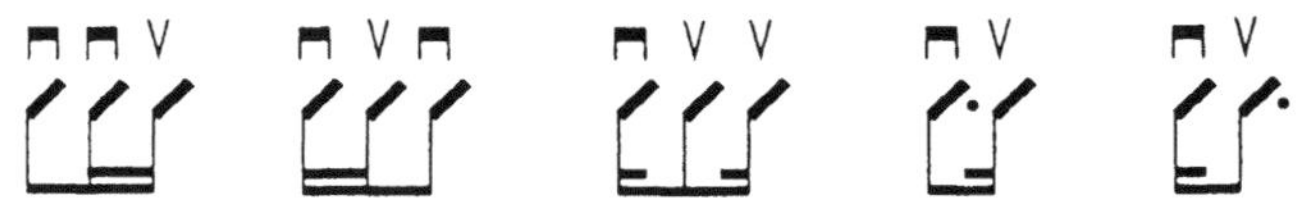

1-& a   1 e&-   1 e - a   1--a   1 e--

Quarter rest: Rest for one beat if the bottom number of the time signature is a "4." If the bottom number is an "8," rest for two beats.

Eighth rest: Rest for ½ beat if the bottom number of the time signature is a "4," and rest for one beat if the bottom number is an "8."

Two-beat rest.

Four-beat rest.

Reading Repeat Signs

Two bar lines and two dots written on the staff are called a repeat sign.

When it appears, go back to where the double bar with the dots on the right was written and play that much of the song again. After repeating, end the piece or continue on.

These are called first and second endings:

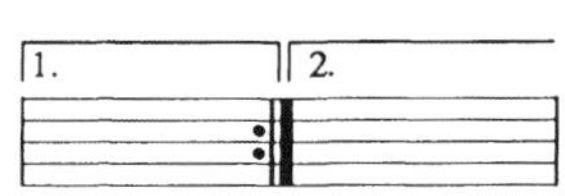

The first time you play through the piece, play the music written under the first ending 1. and then go back to the repeat sign. The second time through the piece, skip the first ending and play the music written under the second ending 2. then continue on.

I
The Blues Progression

One of the most popular forms of the blues is the 12-bar blues progression. The term "progression" refers to a series of chords. "Twelve-bar" means the progression is 12 measures long. The chords used in the basic 12-bar blues are the I, IV, and V chords. The I chord (sometimes called the "tonic") gets its letter name from the first step of the major scale in the key which you are playing. So the I chord in the key of E is E. The IV chord (the subdominant) has the letter name which is four steps up the major scale from the I chord. The IV chord in the key of E is A. The V chord (the dominant) gets its name from the fifth step of the major scale. The V chord in the key of E is B. The following chart shows the I, IV, and V chords in the different keys.

Key ↓ I (Tonic)	IV (Subdominant)	V (Dominant)
A	D	E
B♭	E♭	F
C	F	G
C♯ (D♭)	F♯ (G♭)	G♯ (A♭)
D	G	A
E♭ (D♯)	A♭ (G♯)	B♭ (A♯)
E	A	B
F	B♭	C
F♯	B	C♯
G	C	D
A♭ (G♯)	D♭ (C♯)	E♭ (D♯)

The formula for building the 12-bar blues progression is: four measures of the I chord, two measures of the IV chord, two measures of the I chord, one measure of the V chord, one measure of the IV chord, one measure of the I chord, and one measure of the V chord. The V chord in the last measure is optional. It is played if you are going to repeat the progression. If the progression is not going to be repeated, the I chord should be played again in the last measure.

Written below is the basic 12-bar blues progression. Notice how many measures of each chord are played. The chords in parentheses are the chords that would be used to play the blues in the key of E. Seventh (7) chords are commonly used in the blues because of their dissonant quality. The advantage of knowing the Roman-numeral formula is that, by plugging in the correct I, IV, and V chords, you can play the blues in any key.

Practice playing the following progression strumming down four times in each measure. While it may seem overly simple, strumming down four times in a measure was, and is, a fairly popular technique. Accent beats two and four. Basic chords which are commonly used are drawn on the next page.

Basic Chords

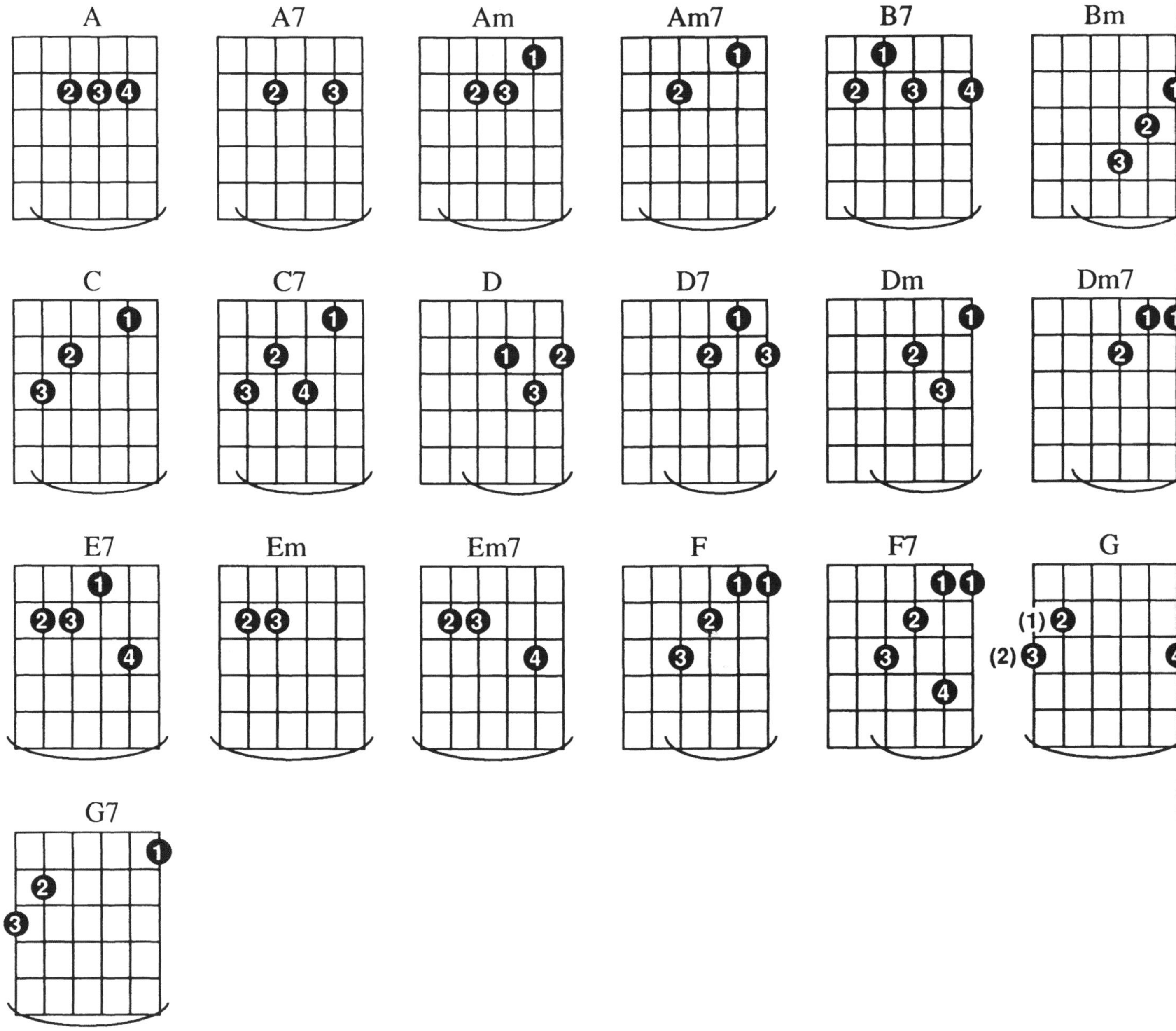

The next progression is a very common variation of the blues. The IV chord has been added in the second measure. Practice strumming this progression. Use the strum pattern which is written in the first measure to play every measure. This strum pattern works well when playing the accompaniment for blues songs in 4/4.

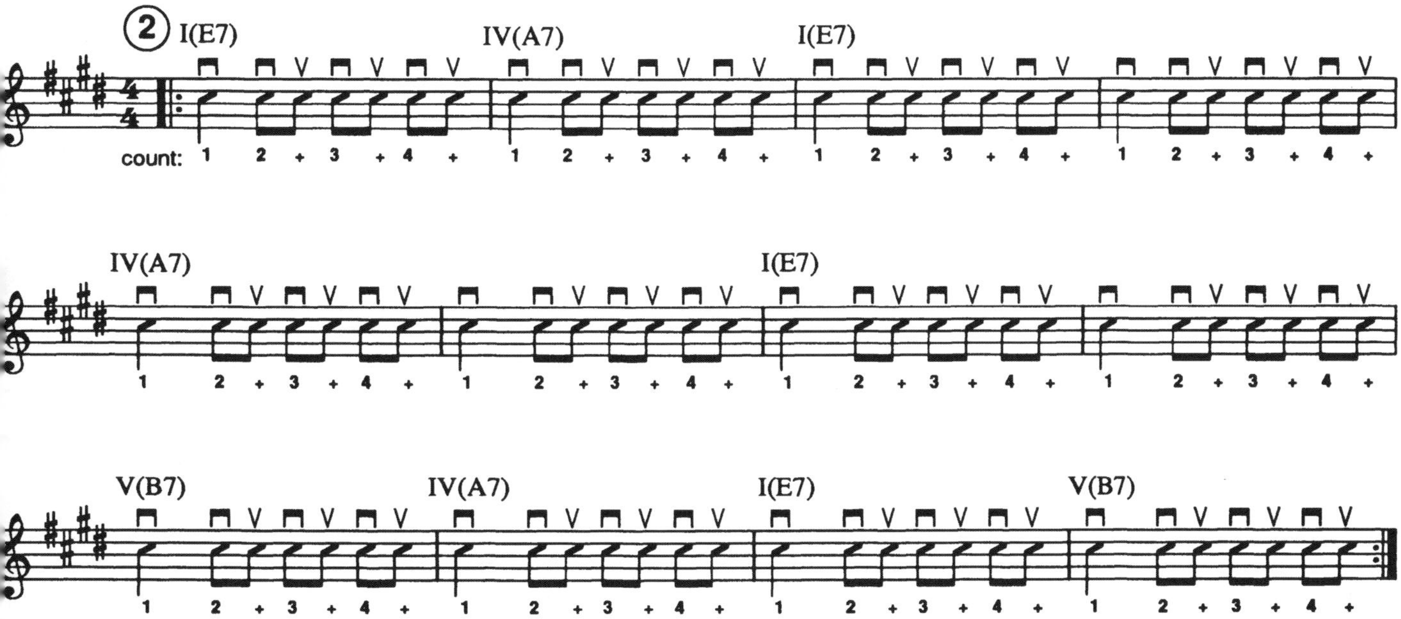

Practice the following blues progression in the key of A. In each measure, use the strum pattern which is written in the first measure. This is another strum pattern which works well to accompany songs in 4/4.

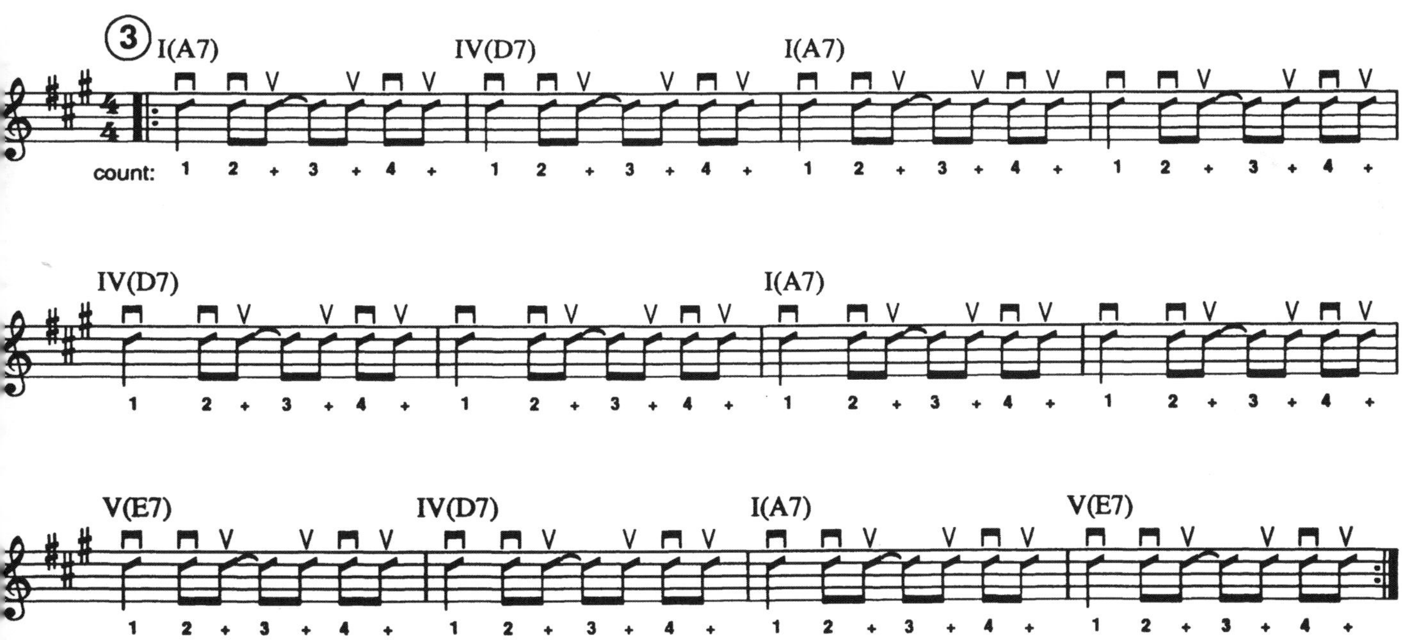

Practice strumming the chords to the following blues song. Use any of the strum patterns which are written below. Each pattern works for 4/4 and takes one measure to complete. Once a pattern has been selected, use the same pattern in each measure of the song.

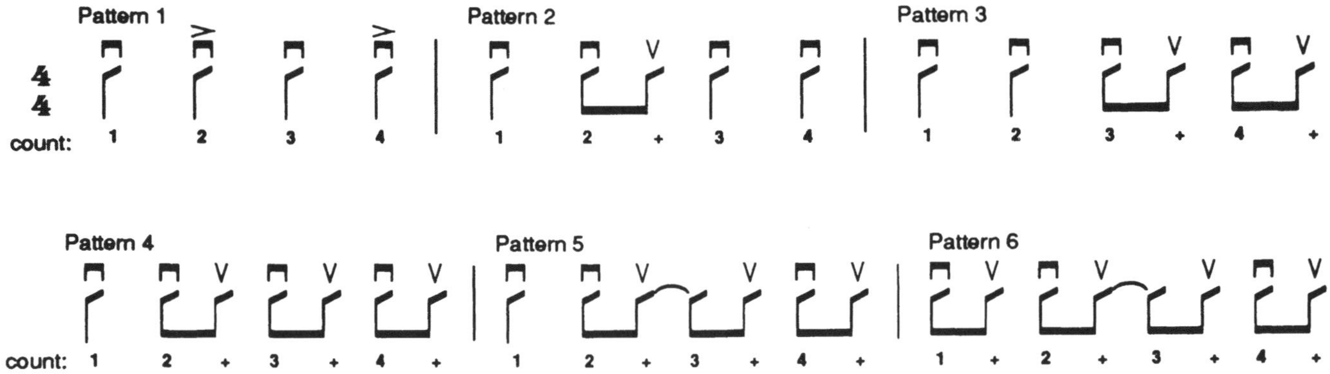

Flat Broke Blues

The next progression is a blues in 6/8. The strum pattern which is written in the first measure is a common strum for 6/8. Use this pattern to play each measure of the progression.

(5)

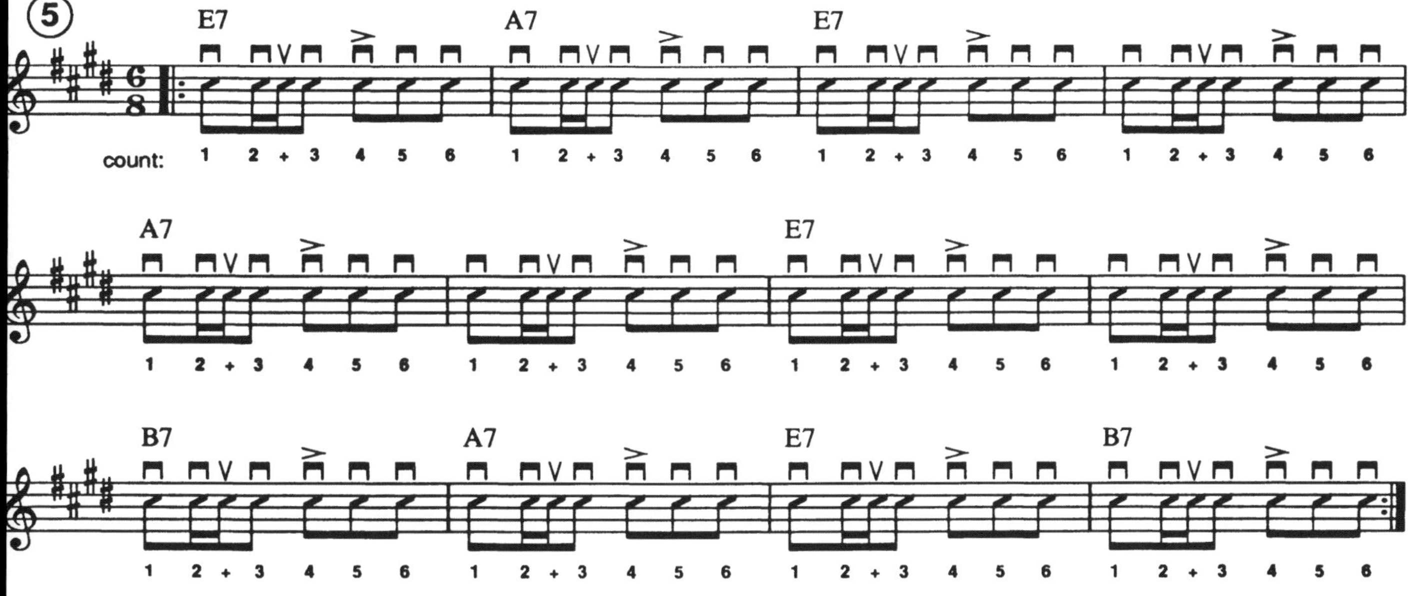

The following exercise is the blues in 12/8 time in the key of E. Again, use the strum pattern which is written in the first measure to play each measure of the progression. This is a common strum pattern for 12/8.

(6)

To play the blues in a minor key, the i and iv chords are minor and the V chord is a seventh chord. Small Roman numerals indicate minor chords. Practice strumming the following blues in A minor. Use any of the strum patterns for 4/4.

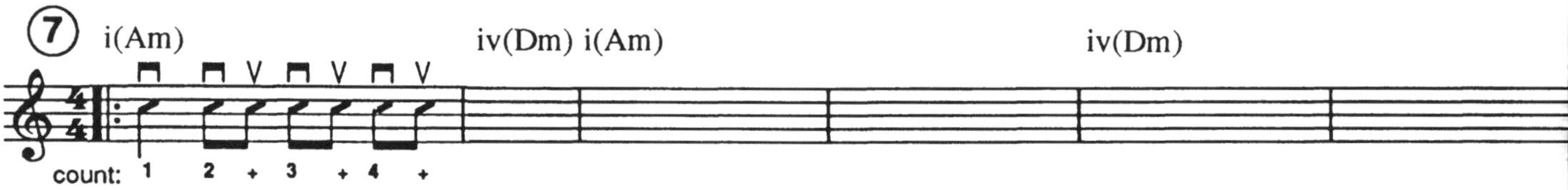

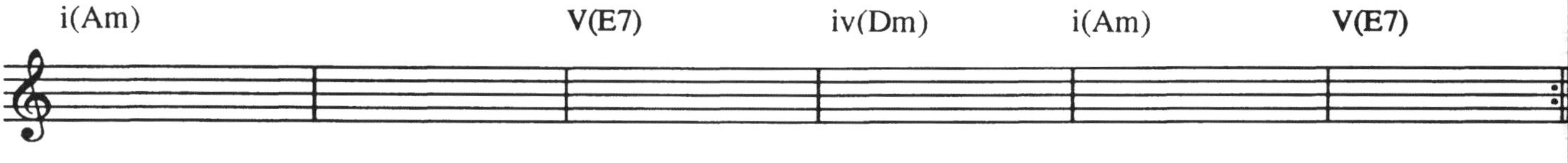

II
Open-String Power Chords

One type of accompaniment which is popular in the blues style involved playing only two strings rather than strumming chords. In rock-style playing, these are referred to as "power chords." Because only two strings are played (the root and the fifth), power chords are written with a "5" after the letter name (i.e., A5). These chords can also be played when the written chord is a major or a 7th chord.

When using these chords, it's very common to play eight strokes to the measure. Like eighth notes, this divides the beat into two equal parts. It is also very common to play these eighth notes with a "swing" or "shuffle" rhythm. This means that when playing the eighth notes, rather than dividing the beat into two equal parts, the beat is divided into a long–short pattern. The eighth notes will sound more like a one-beat triplet with the middle note tied: (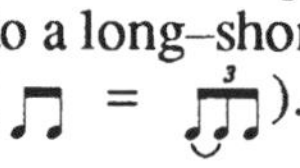).

To get the feel of this rhythm, you could think of the melody to the "Battle Hymn of the Republic." This is generally sung with a swing feel.

The next few examples show how to use this style of accompaniment to play the blues. The following example is in the key of A. Unless otherwise indicated, use the swing rhythm on all of the examples and songs in this book.

In the following exercise, the first two notes which are played together are the A power chord. It's common to do a variation on the power chord by moving the top note. The following exercise uses this variation on the power chord.

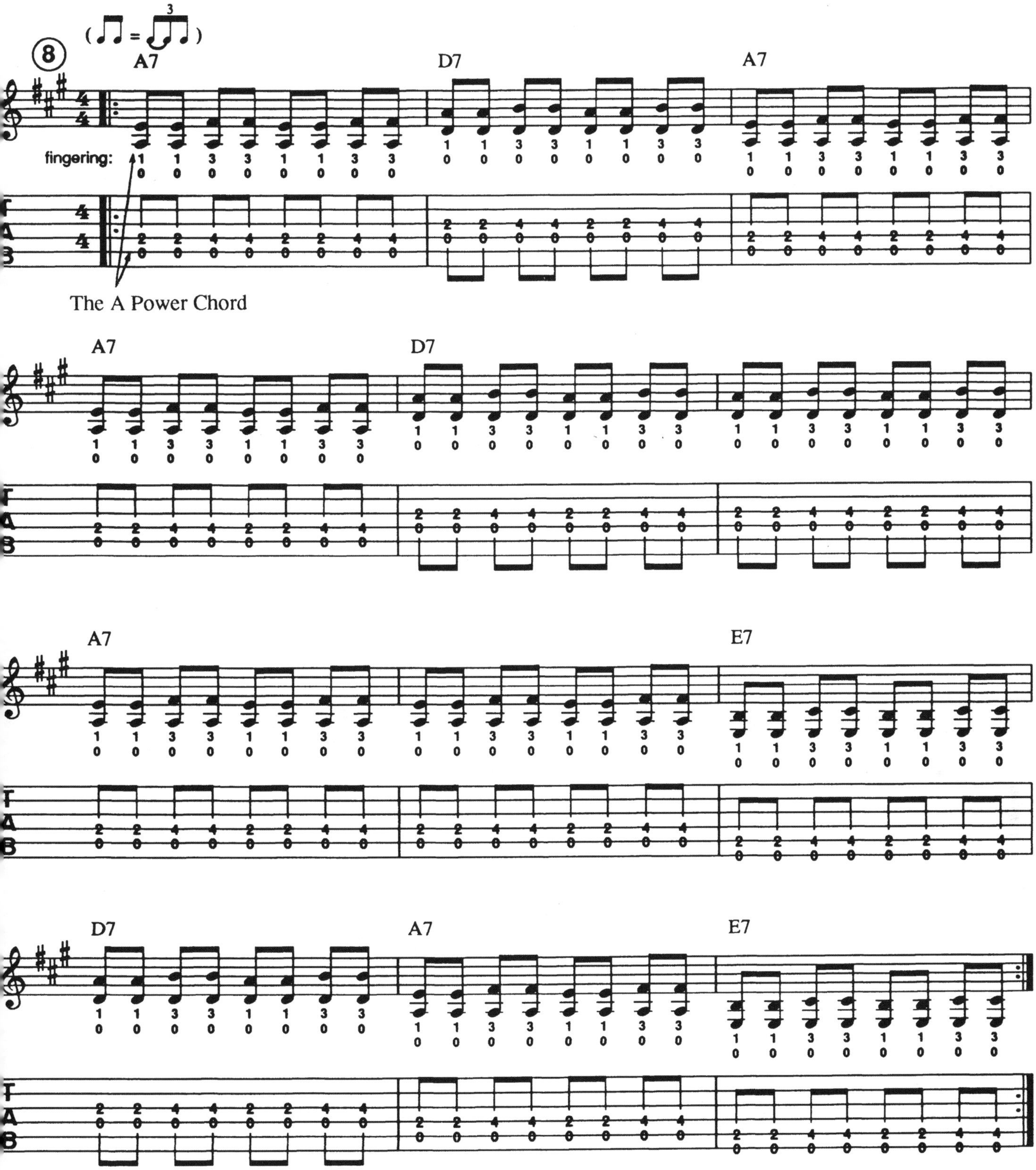

The next example shows a common variation on the power chord.

Play the next example which shows another variation on this technique. Again, use the shuffle rhythm and watch the fingering.

Play the following two songs using the double-string, or "power-chord" style of accompaniment. The vocal melody is written in the standard notation, and the guitar accompaniment is written in standard notation and tablature. Use the shuffle rhythm on both songs.

One More Day Of Workin'

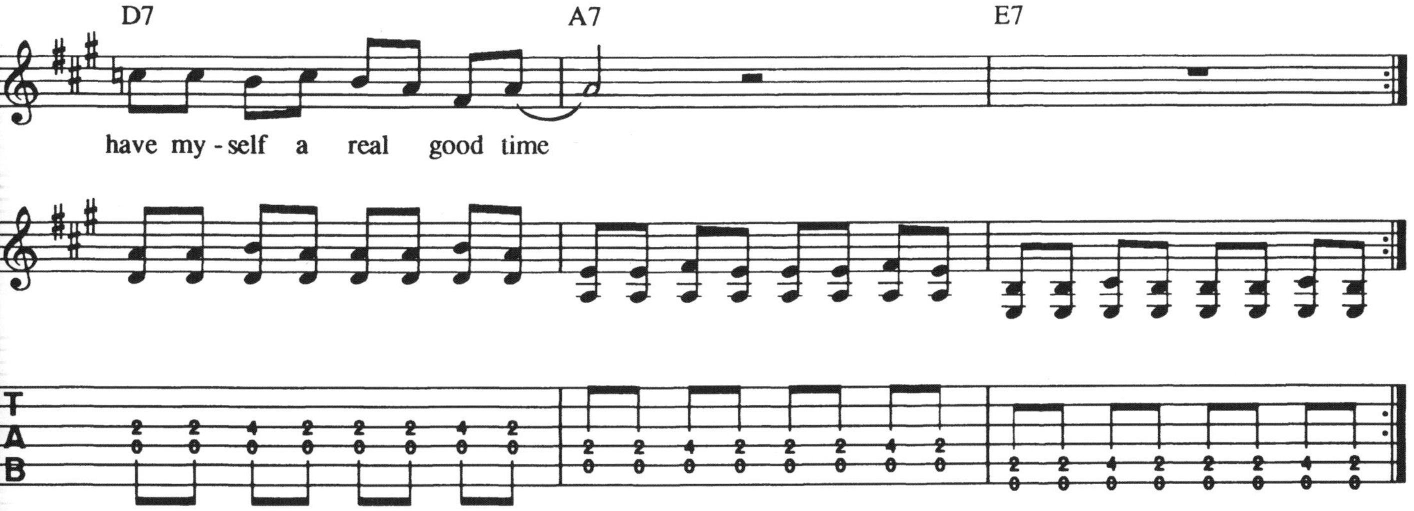

(Additional lyrics)

2. One more day of workin',
   then I'll go out on the town.
   One more day of workin',
   then I'll go out on the town.
   Spendin' all my money,
   so I can start another round.

Dark Clouds

12

III
Moveable Power Chords

Power chords (two-string chords) can also be played without using open strings. The following diagram shows a power chord which can be played anywhere on the guitar neck. The note with the "R" pointing to it is the root. The letter name of this note will be the letter name of he power chord. When playing this chord, play only the strings which have fingers on them.

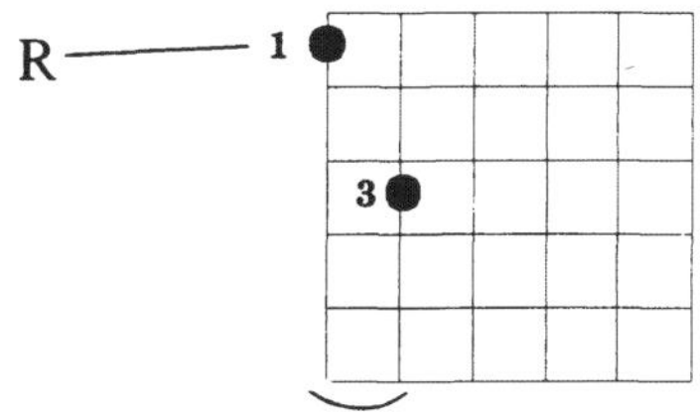

The following chart shows the names of the notes (roots) on the sixth string and the fret numbers in which they are played.

0	1	3	5	7	8	10	12	Fret
E	F	G	A	B	C	D	E	Root name

Power chords may be played on any step of the scale. For example, B5 would have the root in the 7th fret.

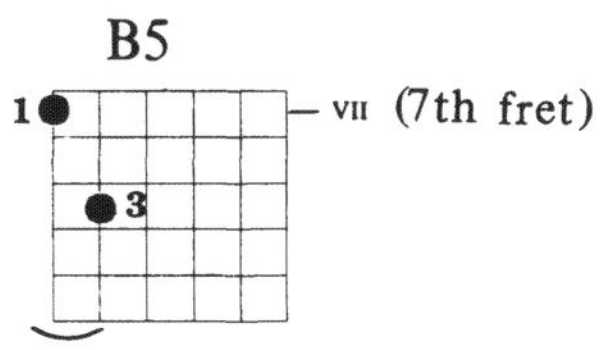

To sharp a power chord, move it up one fret; to flat a power chord, move it down one fret.

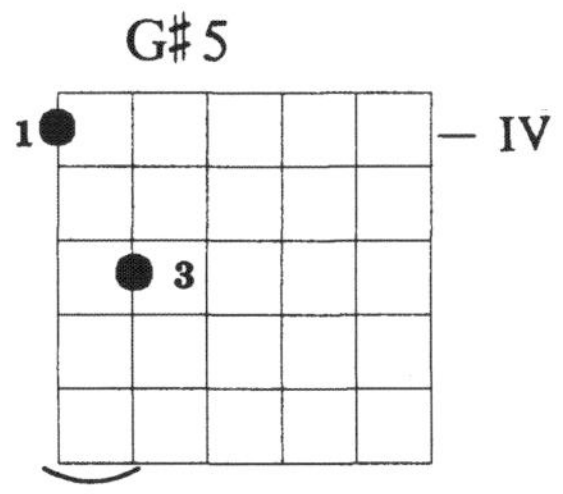

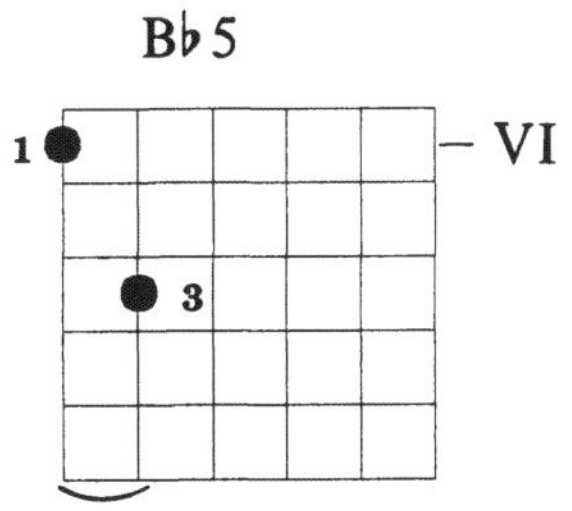

Play the following exercise using power chords with their roots on the sixth string. Remember to play only two strings. Using a pick or your thumb, play only downstrokes. Play eight strokes in a measure (two strokes to each beat).

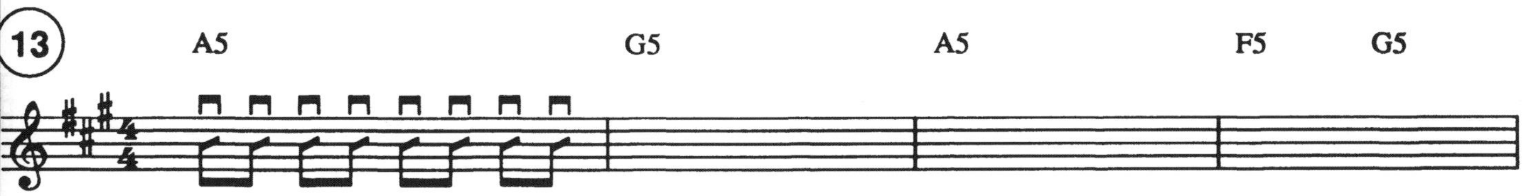

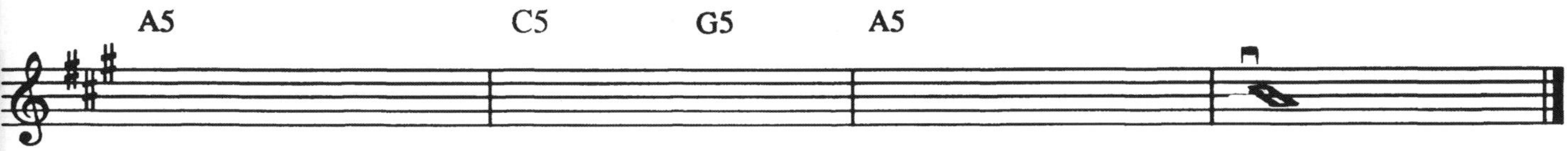

A power chord may also have its root on the fifth string. The following diagram shows the fingering for this type of power chord.

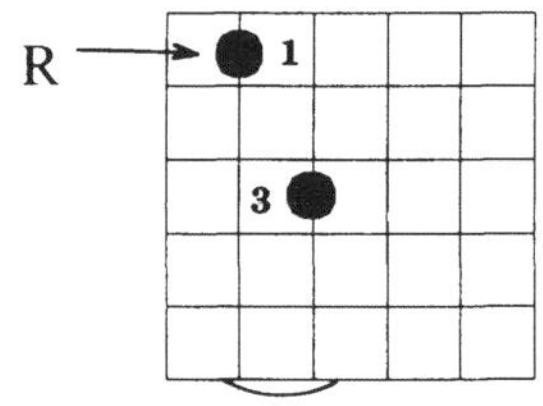

The following chart shows the fret numbers for the root names on the fifth string.

0	2	3	5	7	8	10	12	Fret
A	B	C	D	E	F	G	A	Root name

Drawn below are two examples of power chords with their roots on the fifth string.

C5

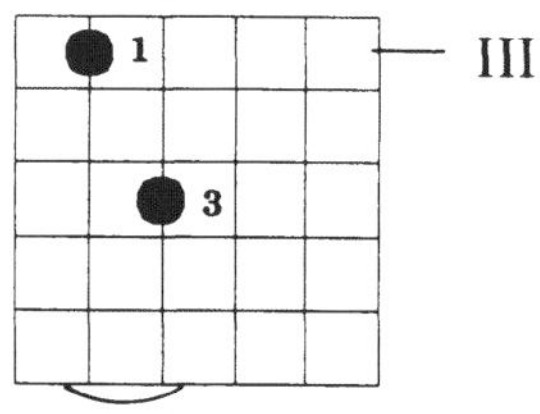

E♭5

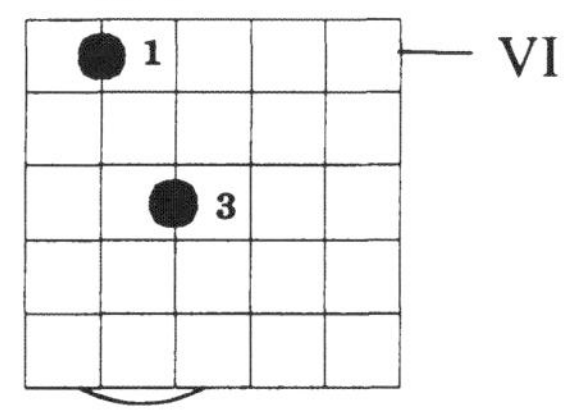

As with the other power chords, sharp the chord by moving the pattern up one fret, and flat the chord by moving it down one fret.

Practice the following progression using power chords with roots on the fifth string.

14

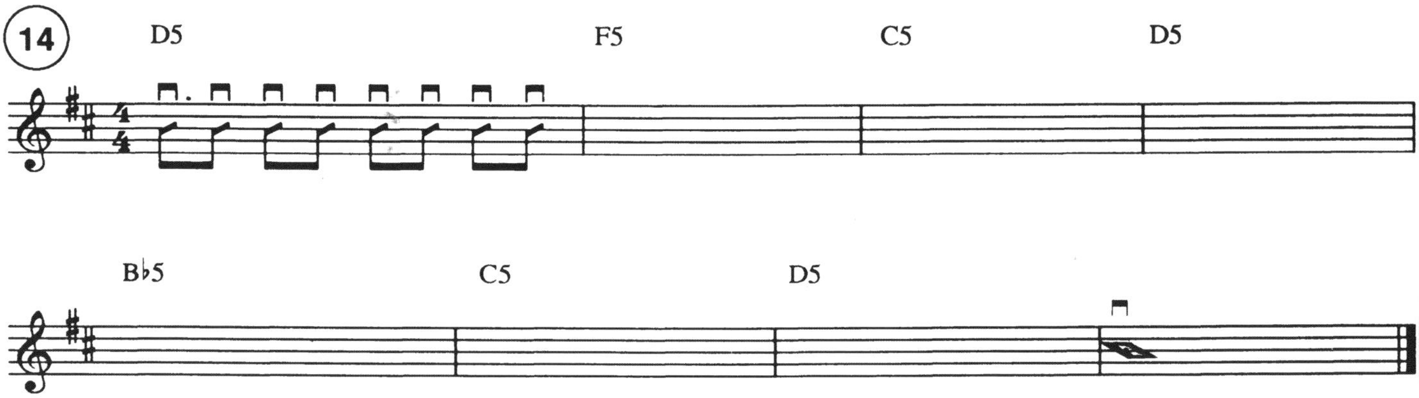

Play the following blues progression which uses power chords with their roots on the sixth and fifth strings. By combining the two different groups of power chords, the different chords can be played close to each other. To help you know which power chord to use, those with the "R6" by them have their roots on the sixth string, and those with their roots on the fifth string are indicated with "R5." Play eight downstrokes in a measure.

15

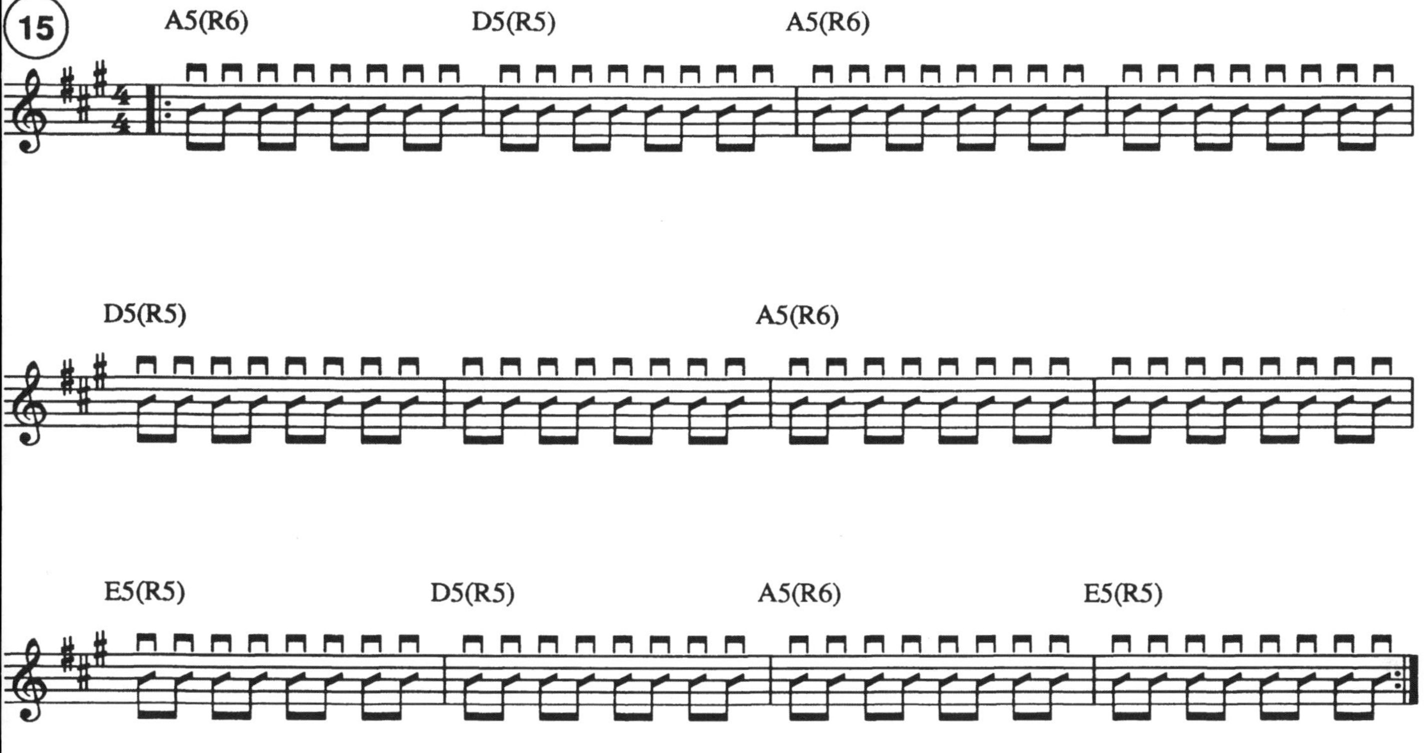

"Moveable power chords" can be modified by adding a finger. The following blues progression is in the key of A and shows how this would be done. The fourth finger is added on beats two and four. Remember, these power chords can be used for the accompaniment when the written chord is a major or a 7th chord.

IV
Barre Chords

When a chord has a finger which lies (bars) across all of the strings, it is called a "barre chord." By using the following charts, you will be able to figure out dozens of chords. The numbers at the beginning of each category indicate in which fret to place the "bar finger" (the finger which lies across the strings). The letters under the numbers show which letter name the chord will have when the bar finger is in that fret.

The first category of barre chords has the root (note which names the chord) on the sixth string. The chart above the diagrams shows the names and fret numbers for those notes (roots). The patterns show how to finger the various types of chords (i.e., major, 7th, etc.). To flat a barre chord, move the entire pattern down one fret. To sharp a barre chord, move the pattern up one fret. Because the B♭ root is in the sixth fret, the B♭7 chord would be played with the bar finger in the sixth fret and by holding the fingering for a 7th chord.

B♭7

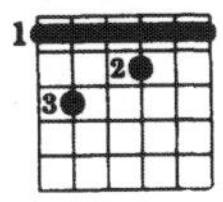

VI

G♯ (major) would be played like this:

G♯

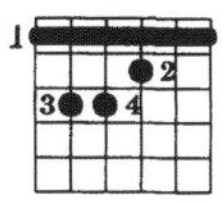

IV

Major chords are those which have only a letter name written such as; G,C,D and A. Major chords may also be sharped or flatted.

The chord patterns which are drawn are chords that are commonly used in playing the blues.

First Category

1	3	5	7	8	10	12	- Fret
F	G	A	B	C	D	E	- Root name (chord letter name)

(Major)

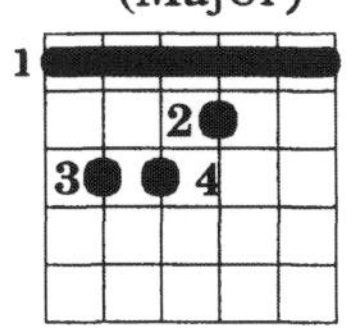

m
(Minor)

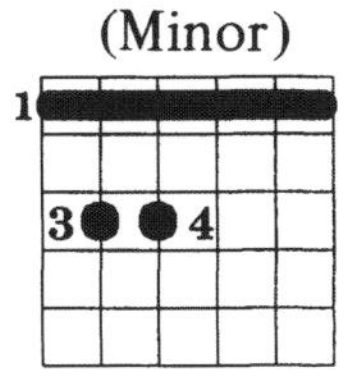

7
(Seventh)

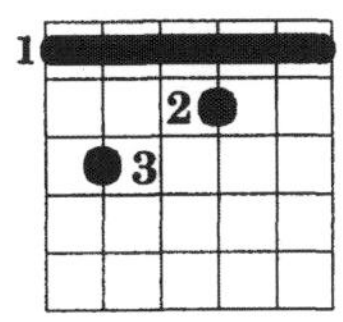

m7
(Minor Seventh)

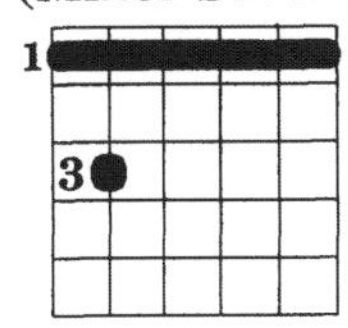

This chord pattern does not have a bar finger. The root is still on the sixth string. The "X" above a string indicates a finger should be tilted and lightly touch that string so that it doesn't sound when strummed. The circle in this pattern indicates where the root would be, but it is *not* fingered or played.

9
(ninth)

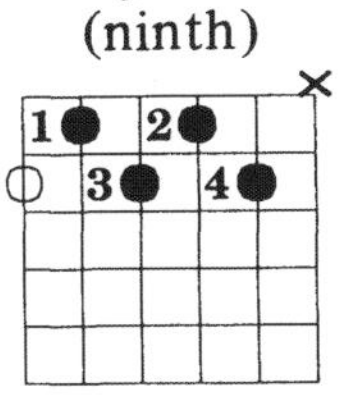

13
(Thirteenth)

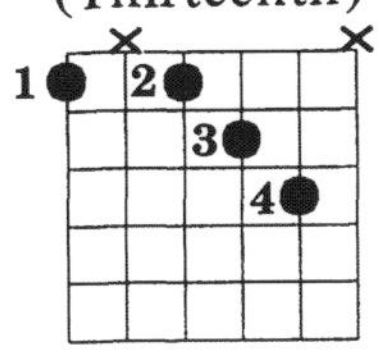

Practice the following exercise using barre chords from the first category. Play each chord as a barre chord. Use the strum pattern which is written in the first measure to play each measure of the exercise.

17

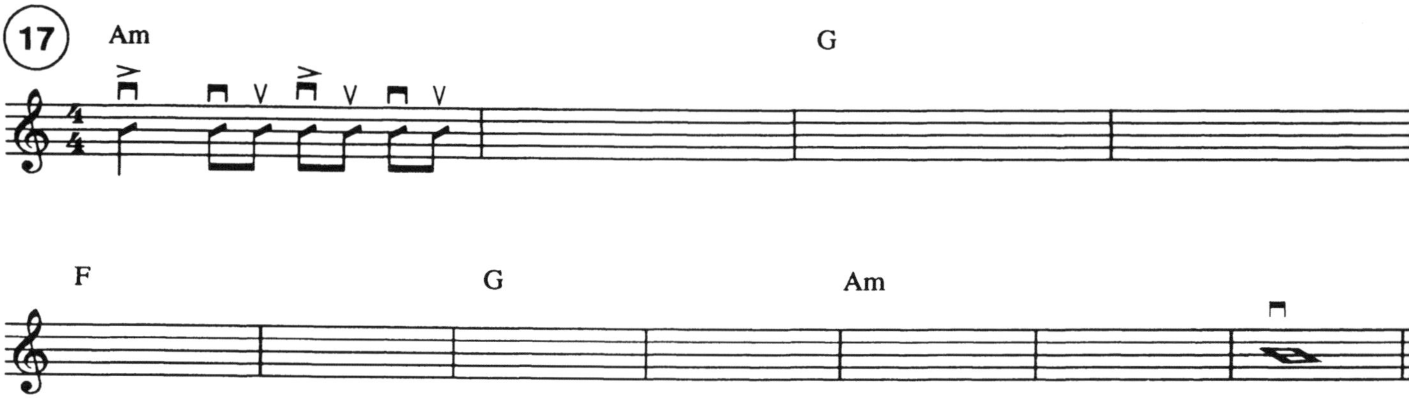

Second Category

By knowing two groups of barre chords, chord changes may be kept closer together and more convenient. The second category of barre chords has the root on the fifth string. In the chart above the diagrams, the numbers show in which fret to place the bar finger. The letters tell what the name of the chord will be when the bar finger is placed in that fret. The diagrams show fingerings for the various types of chords. Because the root D would be in the fifth fret, the D7 chord would be played like this:

D7

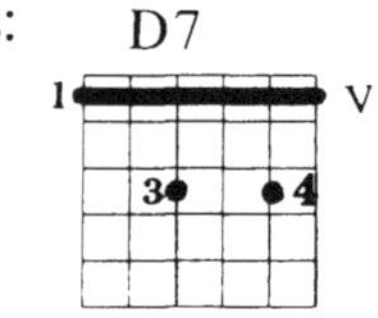

Because the root is on the fifth string,the second category of barre chords will generally sound best if only five strings are strummed.

2	3	5	7	8	10	12	- Fret
B	C	D	E	F	G	A	- Root name (chord letter name)

The "X" above the string in these diagrams means that string is not played.

(Major)

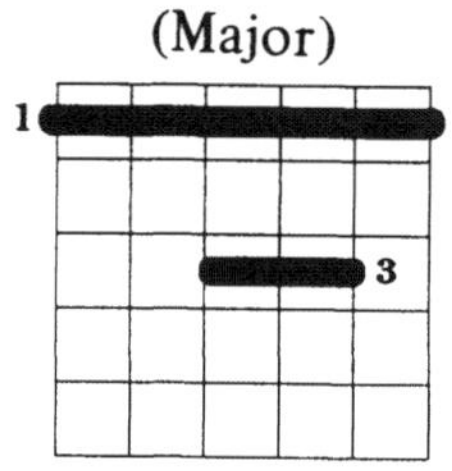

m (Minor)

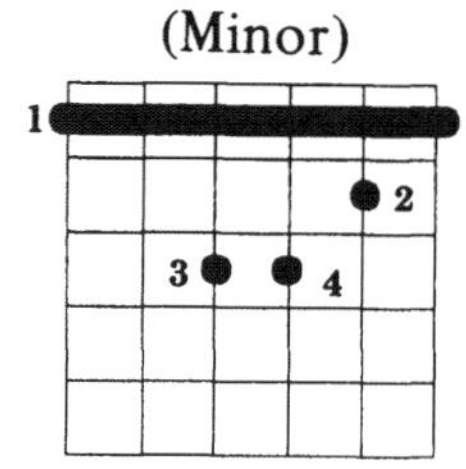

7 (Seventh)

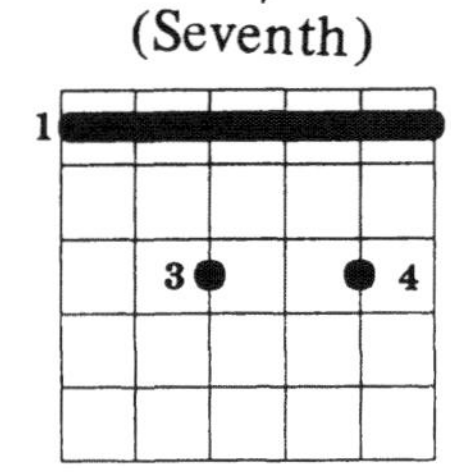

m7 (Minor Seventh)

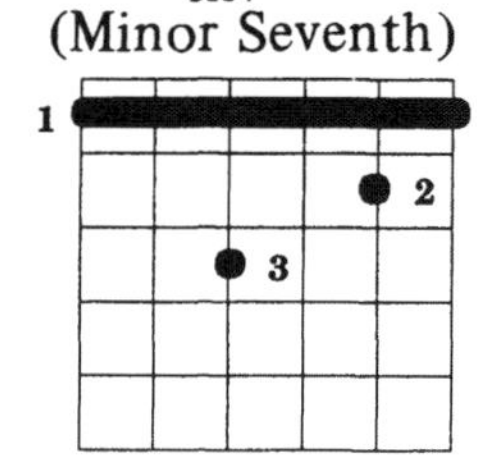

9 (Ninth)

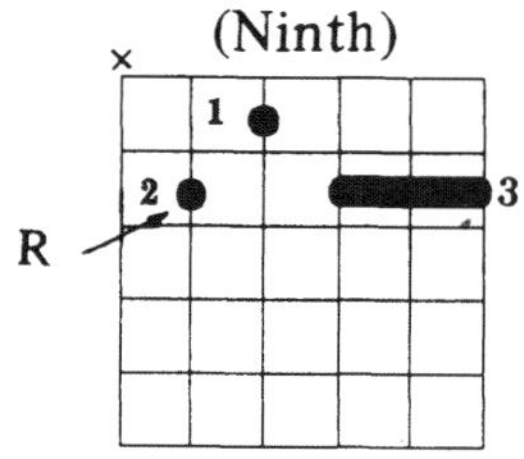

With these patterns, the finger on the fifth string should be placed on the fret number naming the chord (root).

13 (Thirteenth)

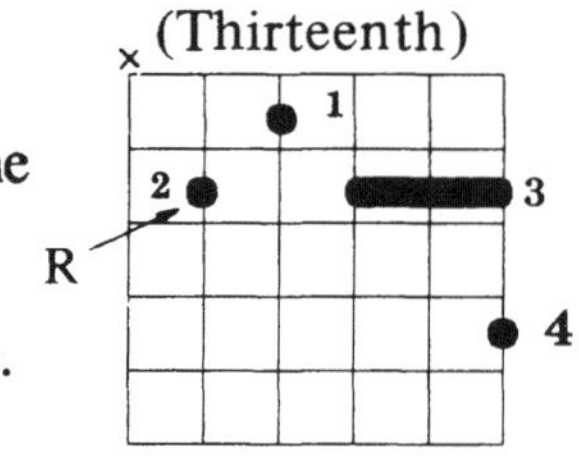

Practice the following progression using barre chords from the second category. Use the strum pattern which is written in the first measure throughout the exercise. Play each chord as a barre chord.

18

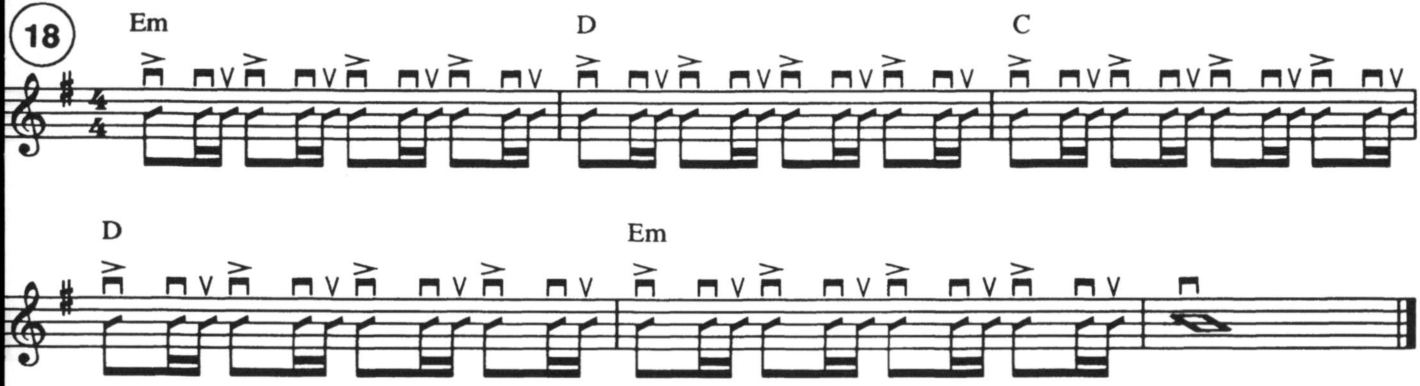

When playing the following blues progression, play each chord as a barre chord. You should combine both categories of barre chords. First, strum down four times in each measure. You could then use the strum patterns which are presented earlier in this book.

19

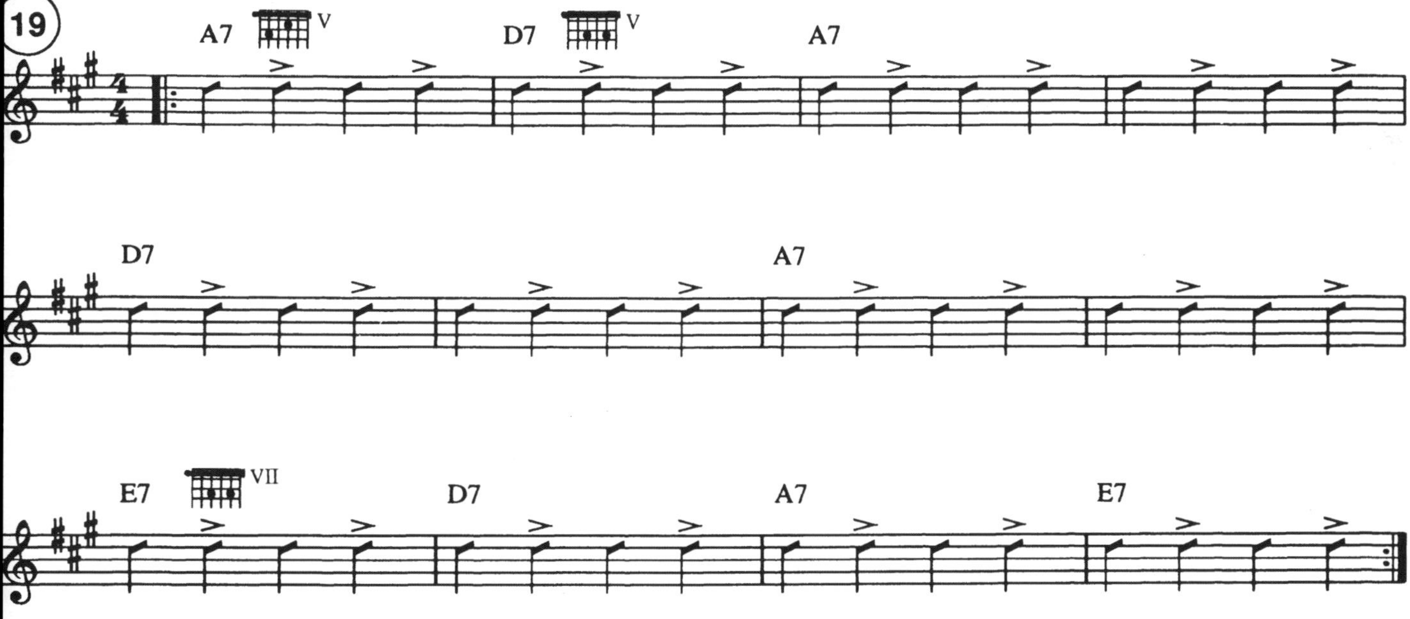

The following pattern for a seventh chord can also move up and down the neck. Like the second category of barre chords, it has its root on the fifth string. The "X" above the sixth string means that string is not played, and the "X" above the first string indicates to tilt the first finger of the left hand and bump the first string, making it dead. The first string is not heard when the chord is strummed.

D7

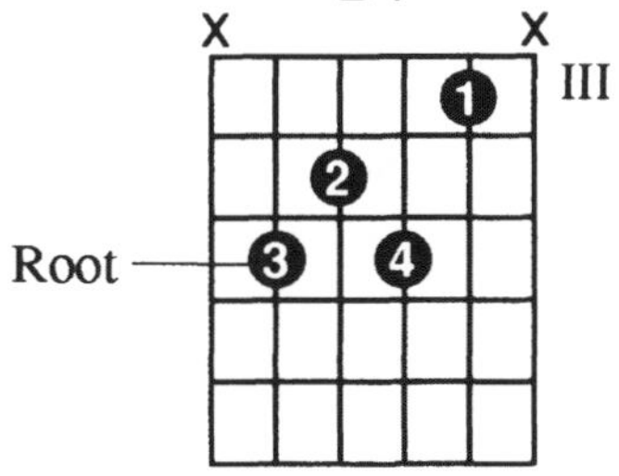

Play the following blues progression which uses this new seventh chord pattern and barre chords.

20

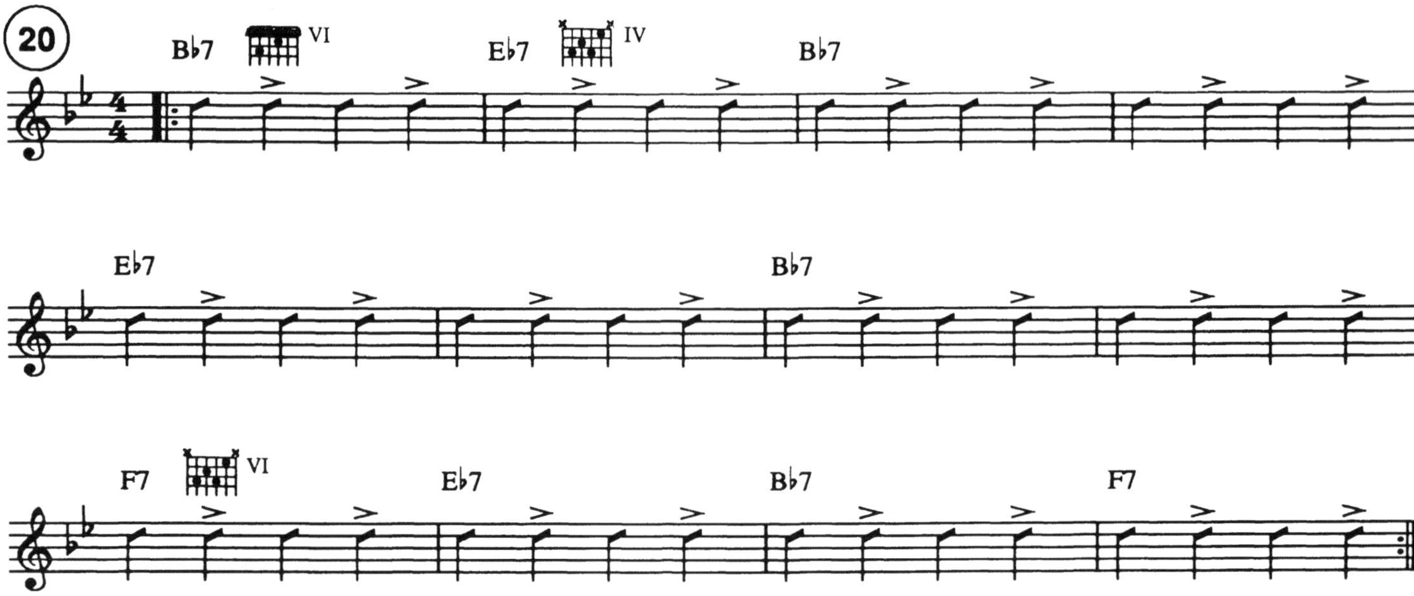

The next two blues progressions (which use barre chords) are variations on the basic 12-bar blues. First, play the exercises strumming down four times in a measure. Then, you could play the same progressions using other strum patterns for 4/4. To keep the chords close together, use both categories of barre chords.

21

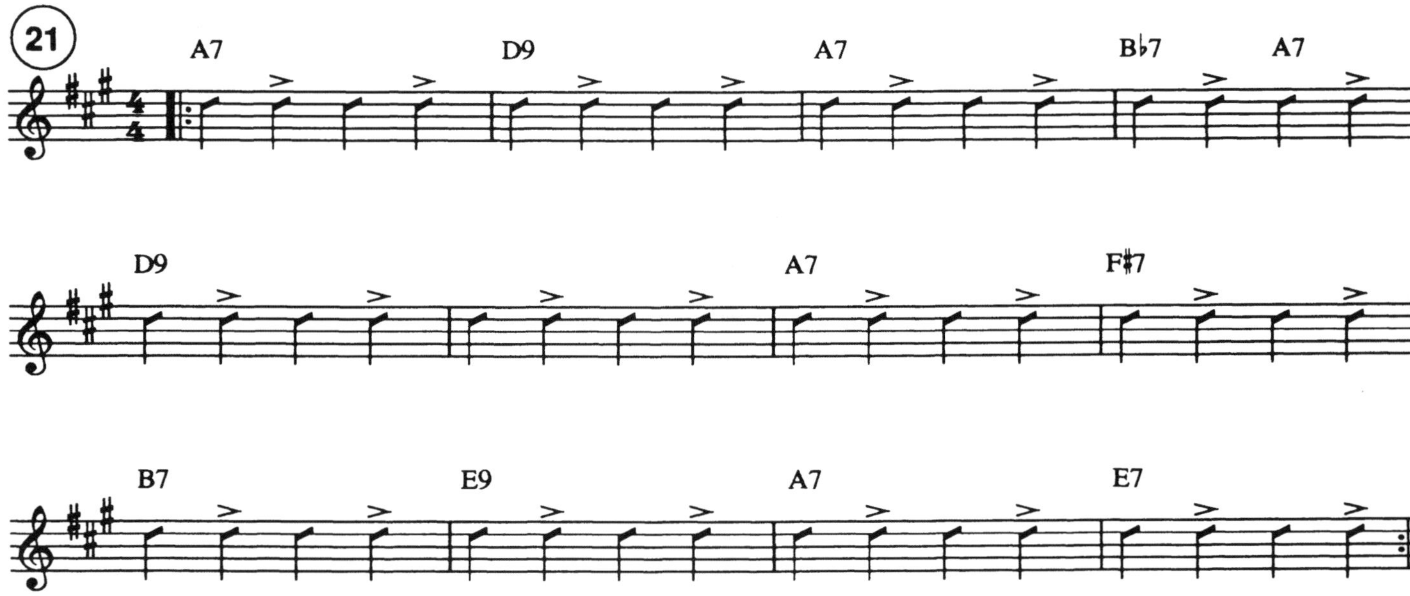

22

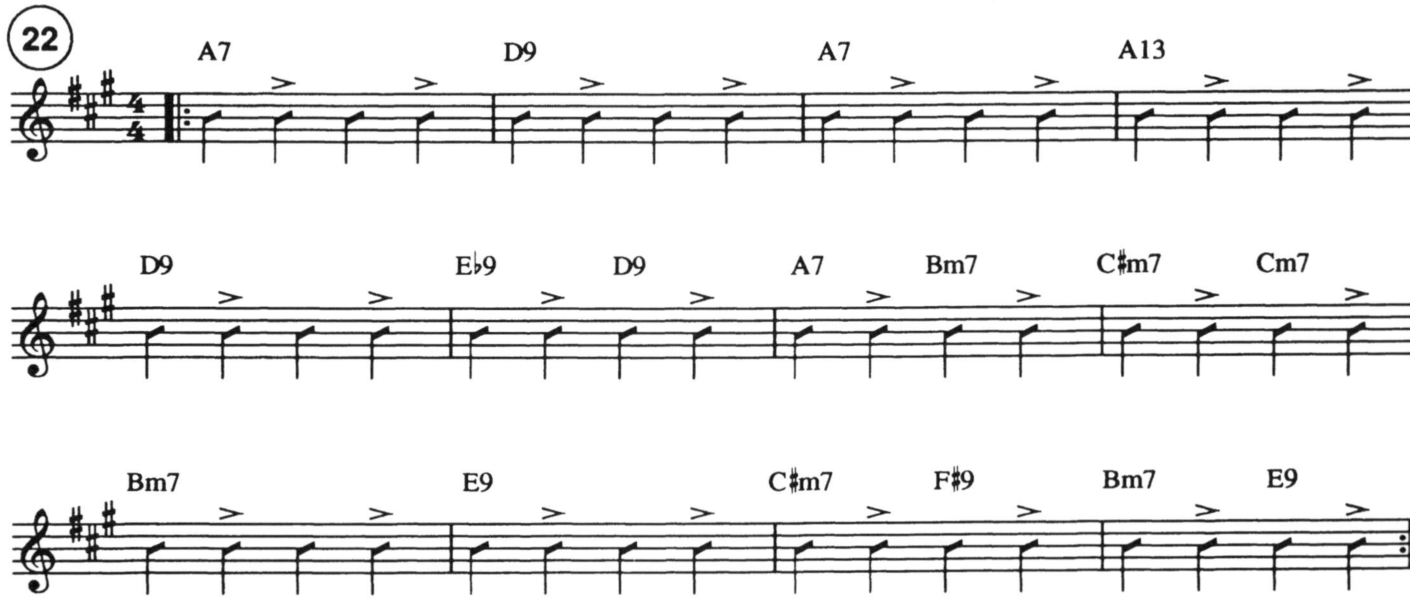

Strum the chords to the following song using barre chords and the new seventh chord pattern. First, strum down four times in a measure, and then practice the song again using the strum patterns for 4/4 which are given earlier in the book.

Pushin' Eighty Blues

Music by Mike Christiansen

Lyrics by Edith W. Morgan

(Additional lyrics)

2. Things I'm hearin', seem far far away.
   Things I'm hearin', seem far far away.
   Like wakin' up on a foggy, foggy day.

3. Things I'm seein' are out of true.
   Things I'm seein' are out of true.
   But you my darlin', I still see you.

4. So take my hand and off we'll go.
   So take my hand and off we'll go.
   Croonin' soft and shufflin' slow.

V
Turnarounds

A turnaround is a series of notes or chords which are played in the last one or two measures of the blues progression. They signal that the progression is going to be repeated or "turn around." They introduce the first measure. These turnarounds are an essential part of the blues. Early blues guitarists had their favorite turnarounds, many of which are still popular and used today.

Written below are many of the more popular turnarounds. Above each turnaround, in parentheses, is written the key for which that turnaround will work. These turnarounds also make great introductions and "fills" for the blues progression. You will see them used in the solos and songs from here on in this book.

Notice the use of the strum bar with the notes and tablature. Strum the chord written above the meas

24

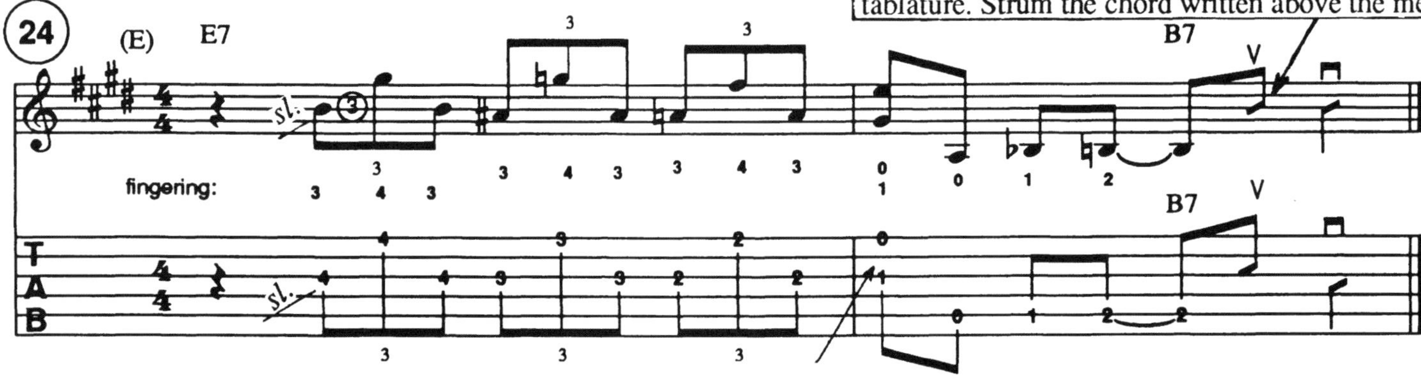

When 2 notes which are not on adjacent strings are played together, use the right-hand thumb and 1st finger (fingerstyle), or the pick and the right-hand 2nd finger (pickstyle).

25

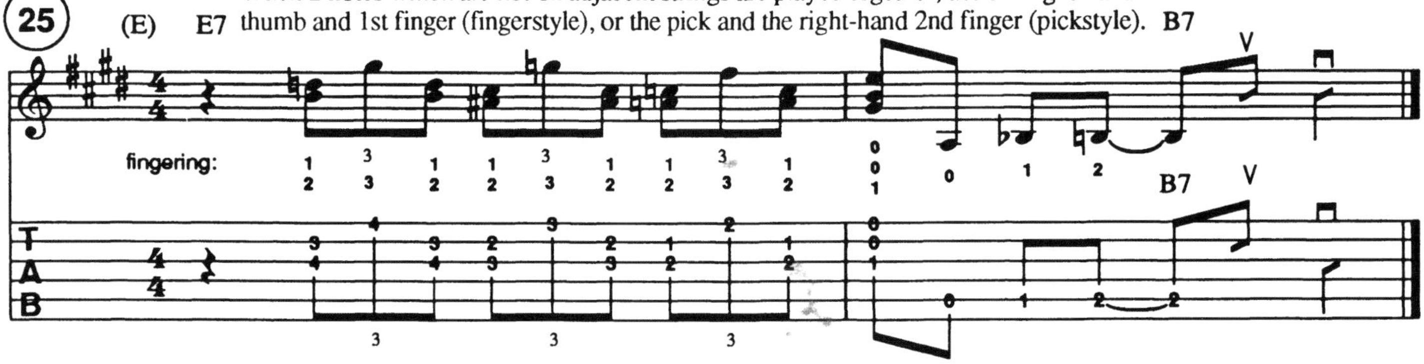

26

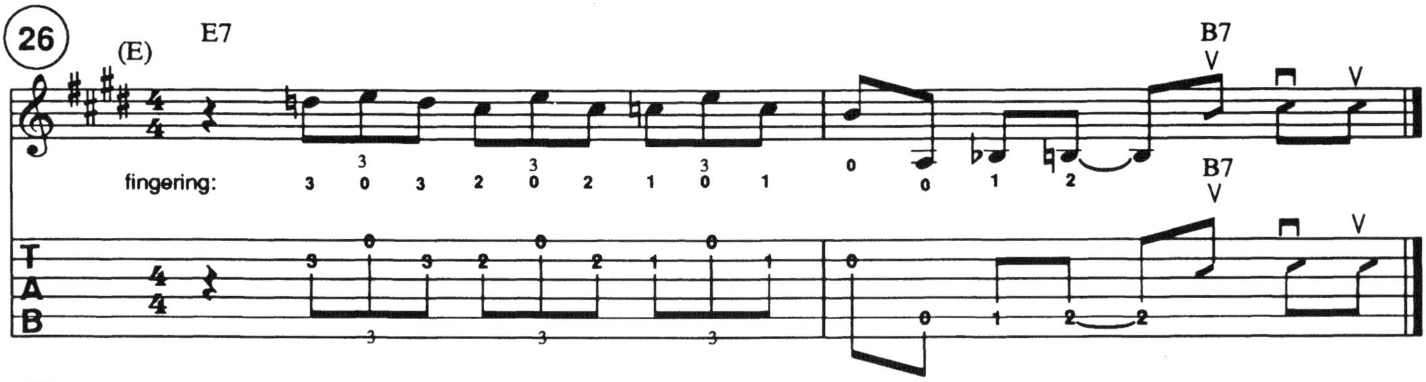

27

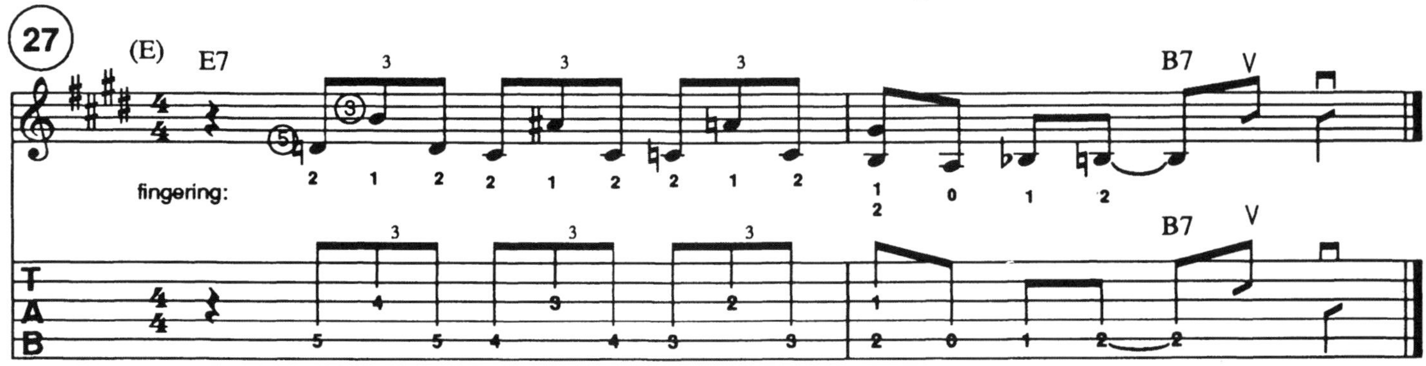

28
(E) E7
B7
fingering:
29
(E) E7
B7
fingering:
30
(E) E A Am E B7
fingering:
31
(E) E
E B7
32
(E) E7
B7
fingering:

33
(A) A7
E7
fingering:
H
E7
H
34
(A) A7
E7
E7
35
(A) A7
E7
E7
36
(A) A7
E7
E7
37
(A) A7
E7
E7

38

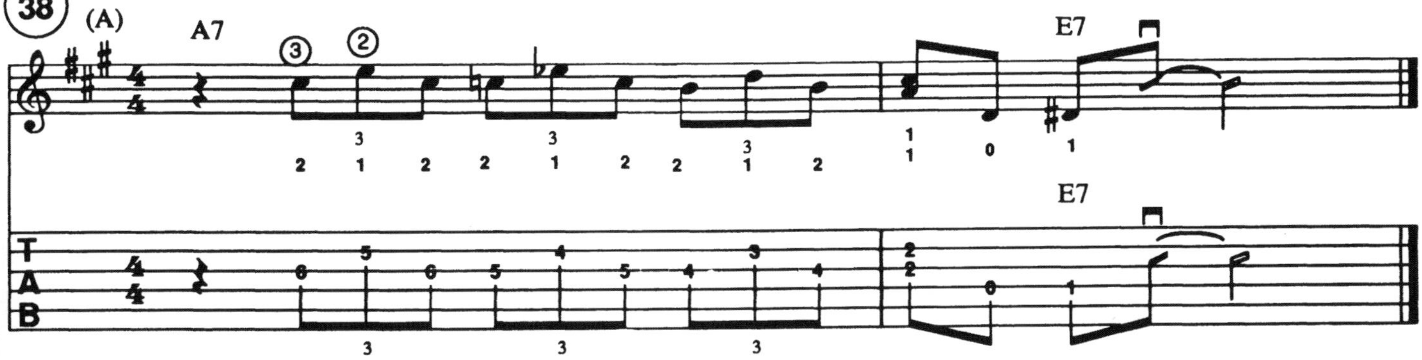

39

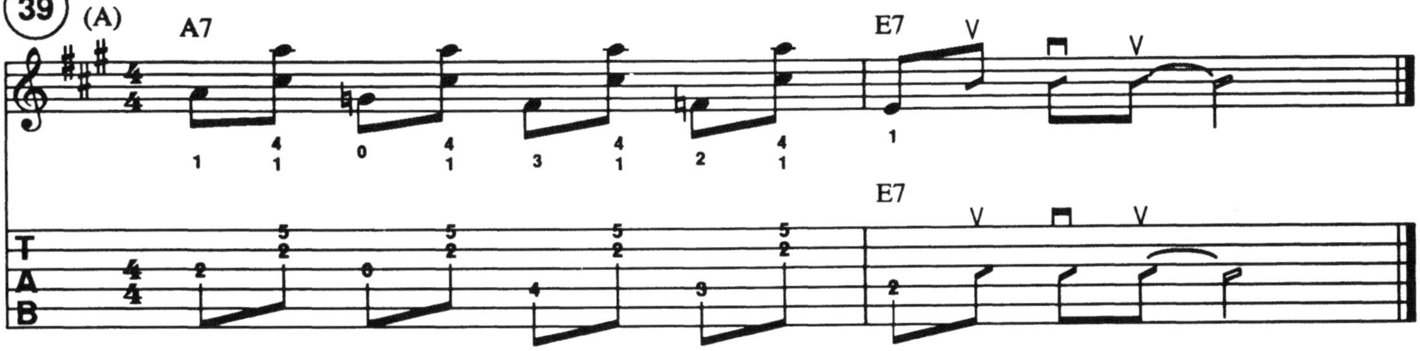

40

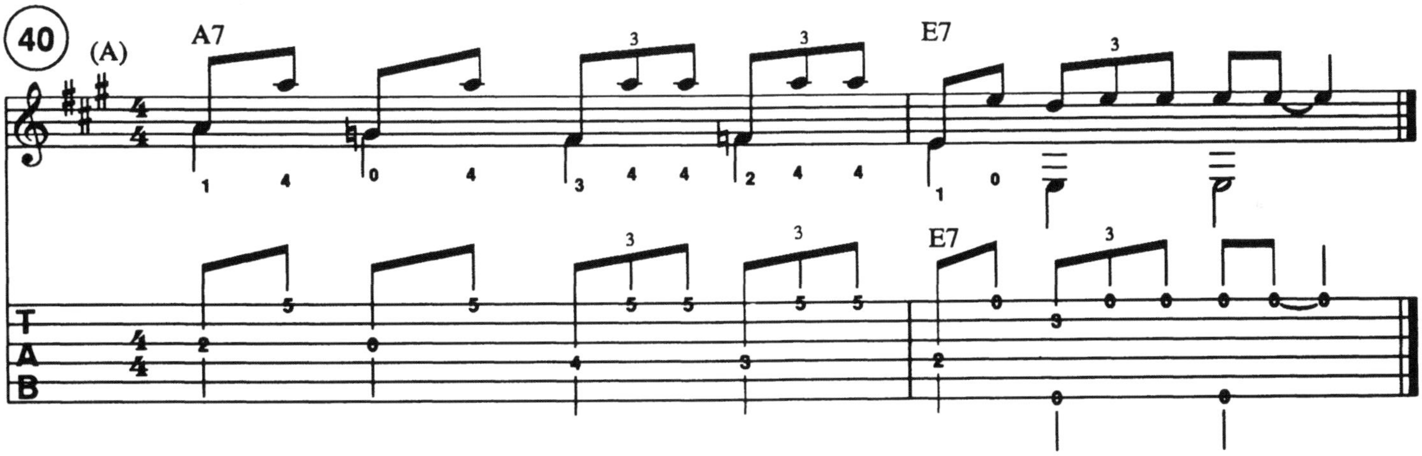

41

42

43

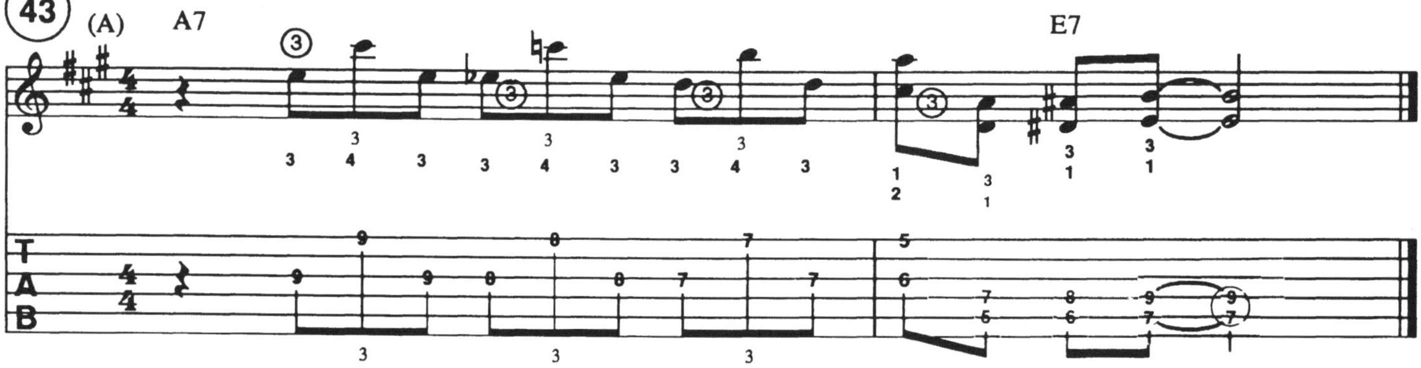

44

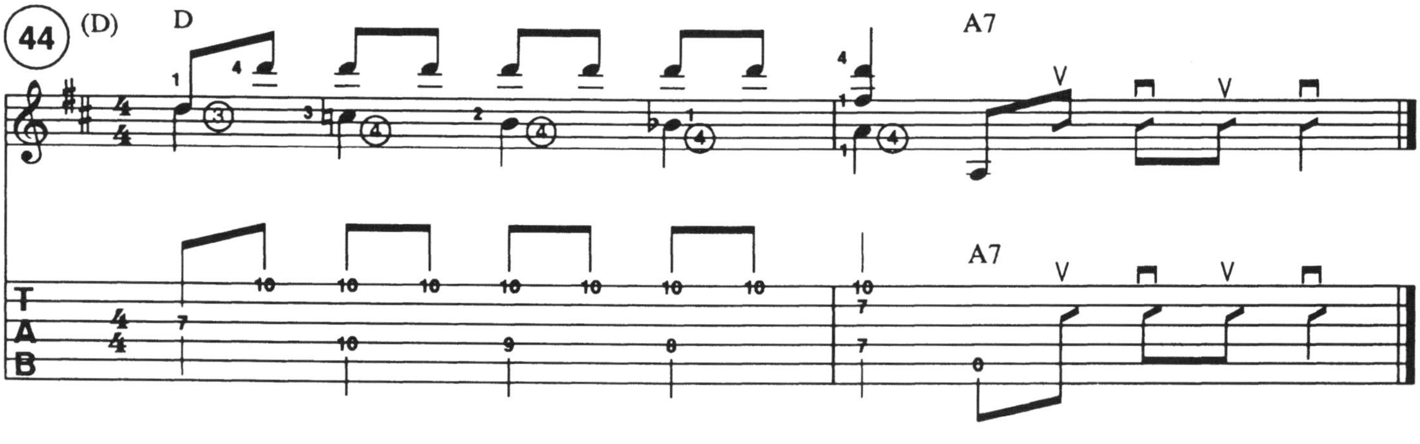

45

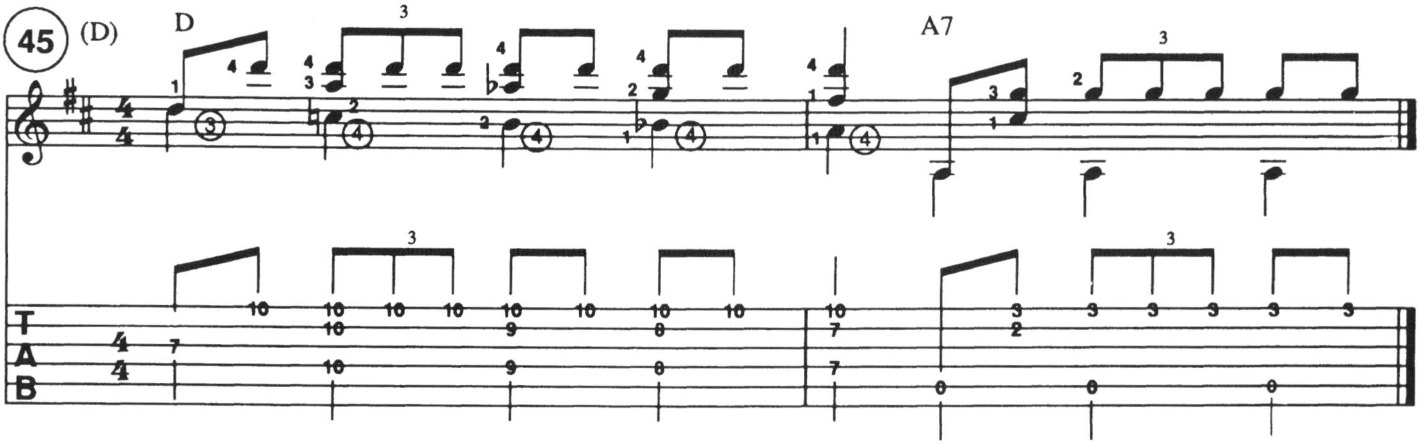

Practice playing the following songs which contain turnarounds. The guitar accompaniment is written in the tablature, and the vocal part is written in standard notation. The turnarounds are written in both the standard notation and the tablature. So they can be easily recognized, the turnarounds have a square around them. Notice the use of the turnaround for the introduction and also the use of power chords in the accompaniment. Use the shuffle rhythm for the accompaniment.

Baby's Lookin' Good

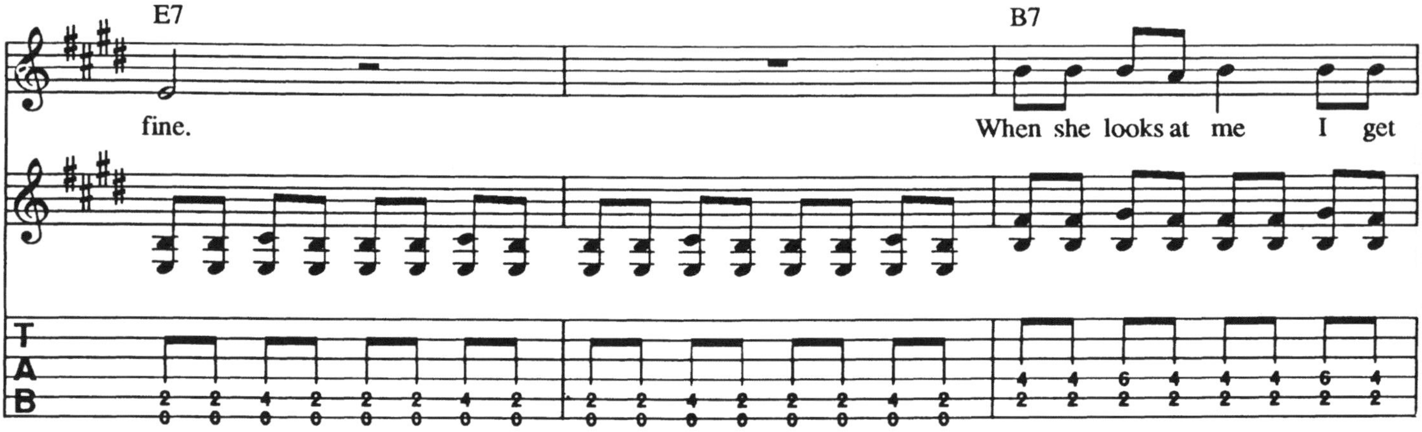

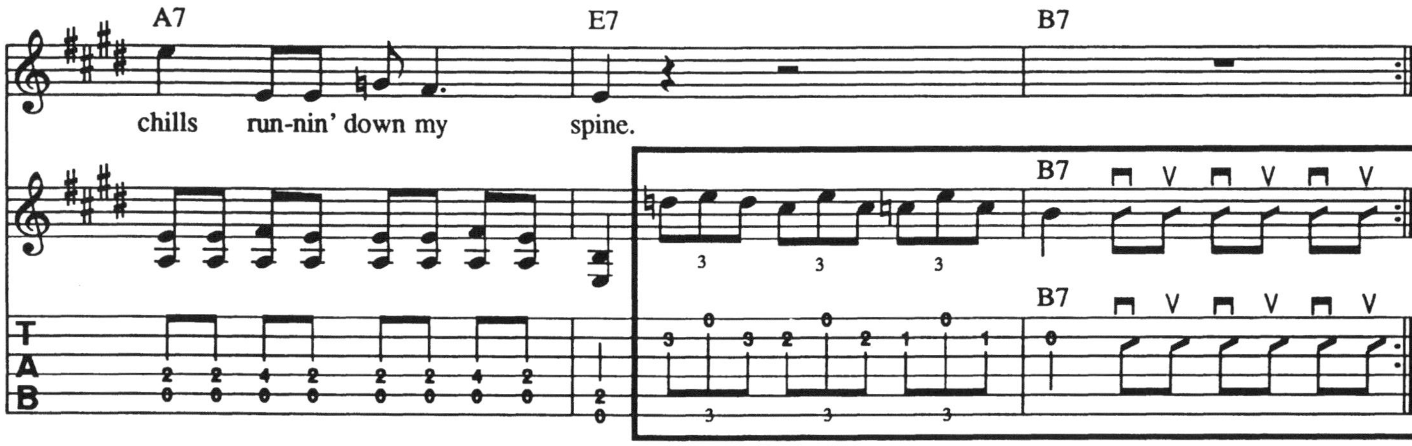

In the next song, the chords are strummed for the accompaniment. Again, a turnaround is used for the introduction.

Baby's Leavin'

47

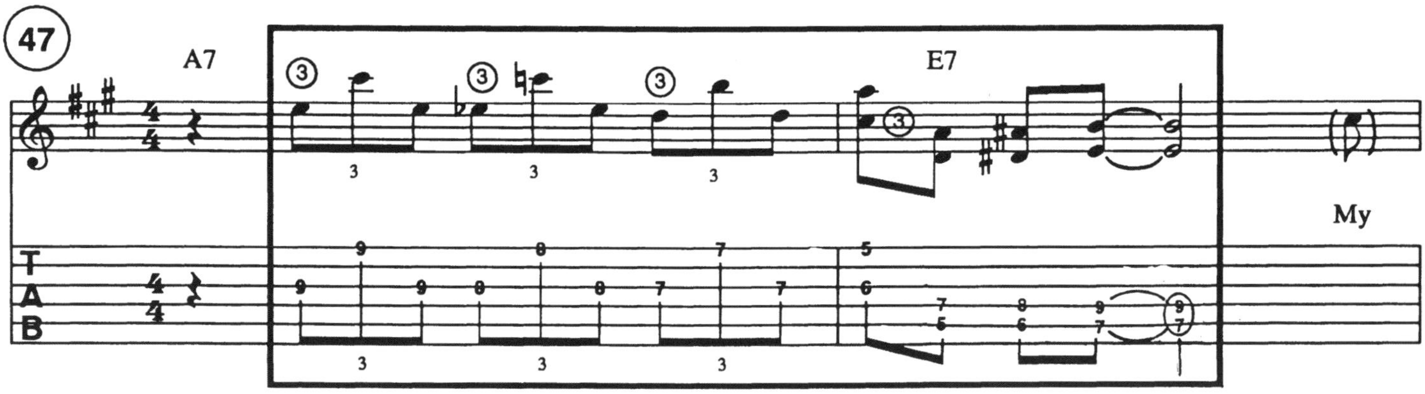

A7
D7
way.
Ba - by said she's leav - in' __
she said she's goin' a - way
A7
E7
D7
said she's not com - in' back could be the best thing thats hap - pened all day.
A7
E7
H

In "Lazy Saturday Blues" a turnaround is used for the introduction, and another turnaround is played in the last two measures. Power chords (double-string chords) are used to accompany the vocal part.

Lazy Saturday Blues

(Additional lyrics)

2. I've got the lazy Saturday blues, I know there's things
   I should get done.
   I've got the lazy Saturday blues, I know there's things
   I should get done.
   But nothins' what I want to do. Just sittin' here and
   takin' in the sun.

VI
Fill-Ins

A "fill-in" is a series of notes (or chords) which are played when there is a pause in the vocal part. The notes used for the fill-ins are often taken from the blues scale. As mentioned earlier in this book, turnarounds can be used for fill-ins.

Practice the next song which contains fill-ins. Again, the guitar accompaniment is written in the tablature and standard notation, and the vocal part in the standard notation. The fill-ins and turnarounds are written in both the standard notation and the tablature. The fill-ins are enclosed in squares, and the turnarounds are enclosed in brackets. Notice that the fill-in happens when there is a break in the vocal part.

Set Me Free

49

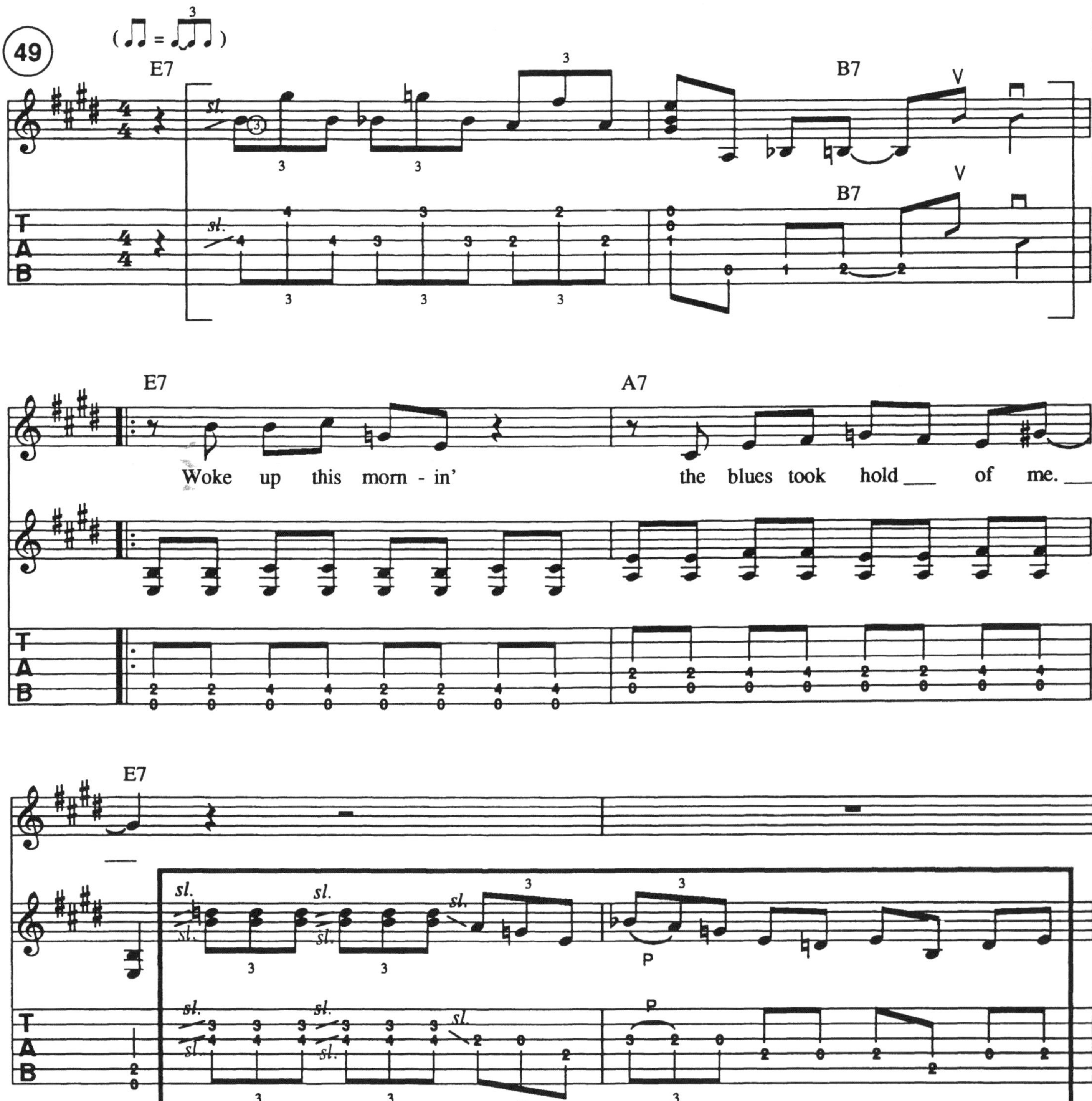

A7
Woke up this mor - nin' the blues took hold of
E7
me.
1/2
H
P
B7
A7
I wish these blues would just leave and set me
E7
free.
B7
E7

The fill-ins in the next song are done by strumming three-string chords. The accompaniment consists of strumming chords. Notice that the turnaround at the end of the song also is done by strumming these three-string chords.

Deadline Blues

It is very common for the fill-in to imitate the vocal part. The next song shows how this would be done. Notice that, unlike most of the other exercises and songs in this book, in the next song the shuffle rhythm is not used for the accompaniment. The beat is divided into two equal parts.

Ain't No Cure

51
A7
D7
I went to the doc - tor
said, "Could you help me
A7
please?"
sl.
D7
I went to the doc - tor
said, "Could you help me
A7
E7
please?"
He said, "Son there ain't no cure
'cause the

VII
The Blues Scale

The diagram drawn below shows the blues scale for the key of E. The blues scale contains the root, ♭3, 4, ♭5, ♮5, and ♭7. The empty circles indicate to play open strings. Below the diagram are written the notes in standard notation and tablature for the E blues scale.

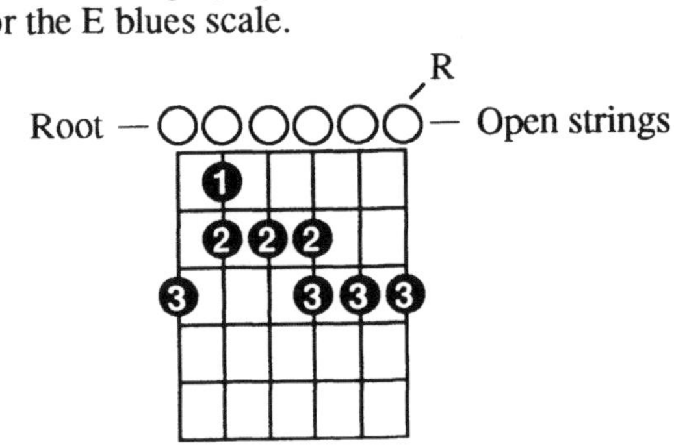

52 When soloing, the fingerings for the scale may change depending upon the order in which the notes are played.

This scale can be moved anywhere on the neck. The note with the "R" pointing to it is the root. The letter name of this note is the letter name of the scale. By placing the root on different notes, you can play the blues scale for any key. When the blues scale is moved up the neck, the open strings on the diagram above would be fingered with the first finger.

The chart below gives the fret numbers for the roots on the sixth and first strings.

Fret →	0	1	2	3	4	5	6	7	8	9	10	11	12
Root Name →	E	F	F♯ G♭	G	G♯ A♭	A	A♯ B♭	B	C	C♯ D♭	D	D♯ E♭	E

To sharp the blues scale, move it up one fret; and to flat the scale, move it down one fret.

The blues scale can be used to solo over 7th, minor, m7, and power chords. To improvise a solo, use the scale which has the same letter name as the key in which you are playing. When the chords change, it's not necessary to change the scale. The blues scale with the letter name of the key can be used to solo over all of the chords in the blues progression.

Practice the following solo which uses the E blues scale. The solo can be played using the fingers, but it will probably sound better using the pick. After you practice the written solos in this section of the book, create your own solos *in several different keys* using the scales. It would also be a good idea to transpose these written solos into different keys.

The next diagram shows an upper extension of the E blues scale. Like the other blues scale, this scale can be moved up the neck and used for other keys.

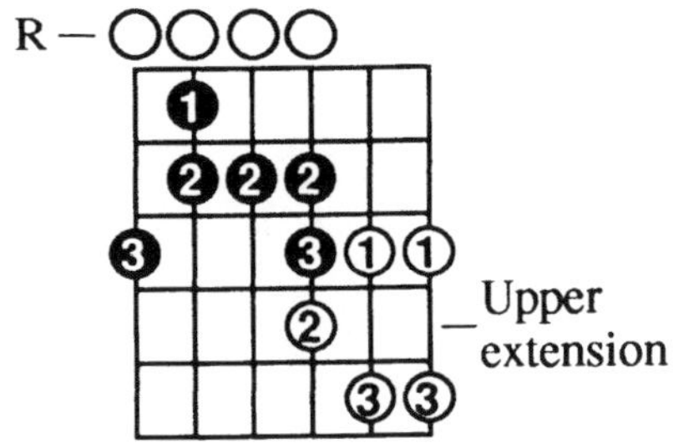

54

The next solo uses the E blues scale with its upper extension.

55

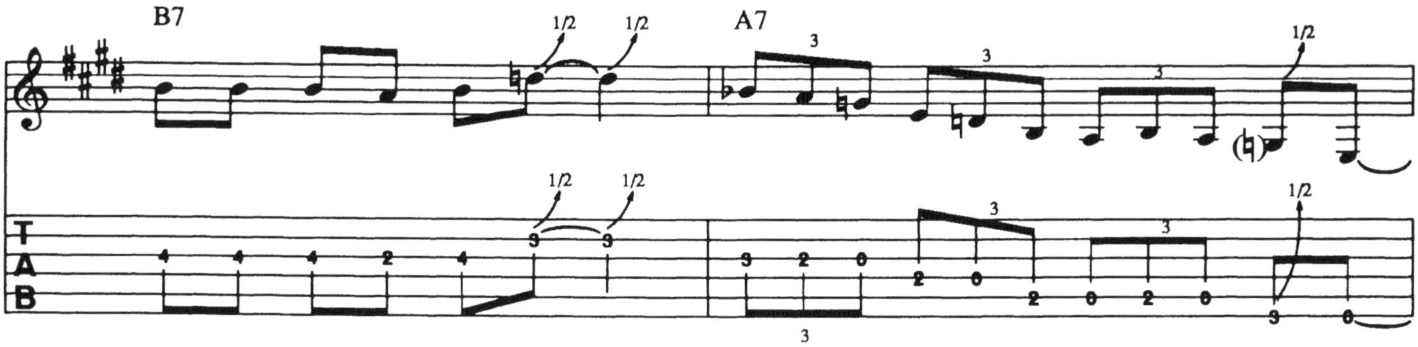

"Swamp Blues" is a solo which uses combinations of the basic E blues scale and the upper extension.

Swamp Blues

56

The next solo uses some variations on the blues scale.

57

The following blues solo uses the basic blues scale in the key of G. For the key of G, the blues scale would be positioned so the root is on the third fret, sixth string.

58

This next solo uses the G blues scale with its upper extension.

The following diagram shows the lower extension of the blues scale with the root on the sixth string.

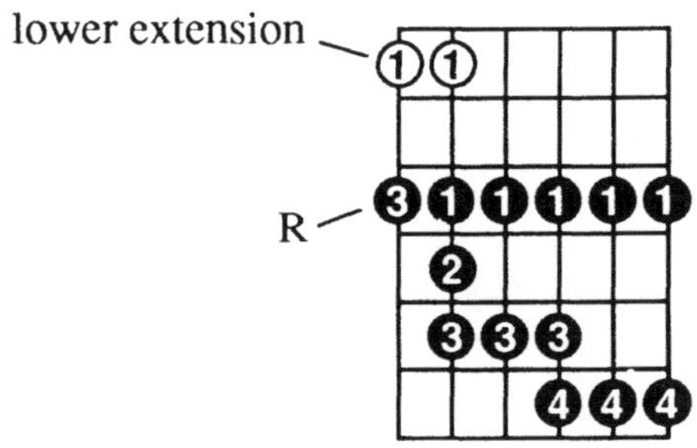

Written below are the notes and tablature for the A blues scale with the root on the sixth string and the lower extension. Because it is the *A* blues scale, the scale is positioned with the root on the sixth string, fifth fret.

60

Practice the following solo which uses the lower extension of the A blues scale with the root on the sixth string, third fret.

61

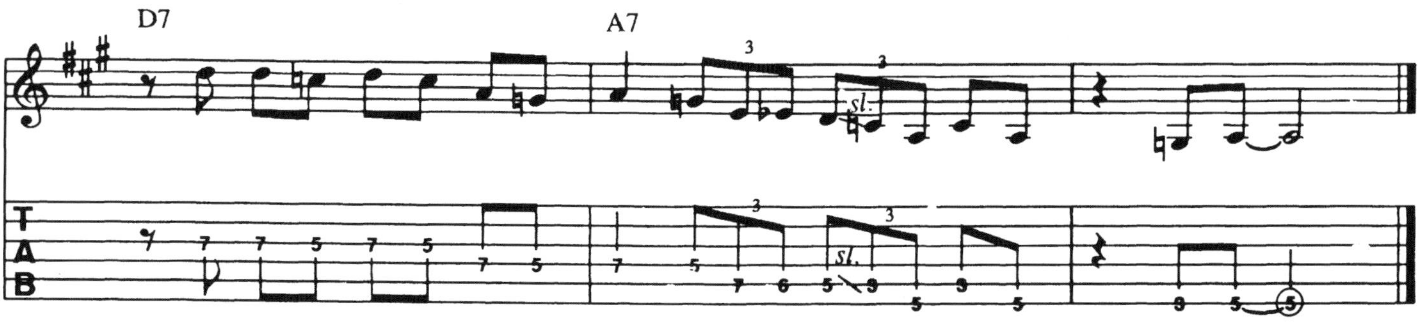

The next diagram shows the lower and upper extensions of the blues scale with the root on the sixth string.

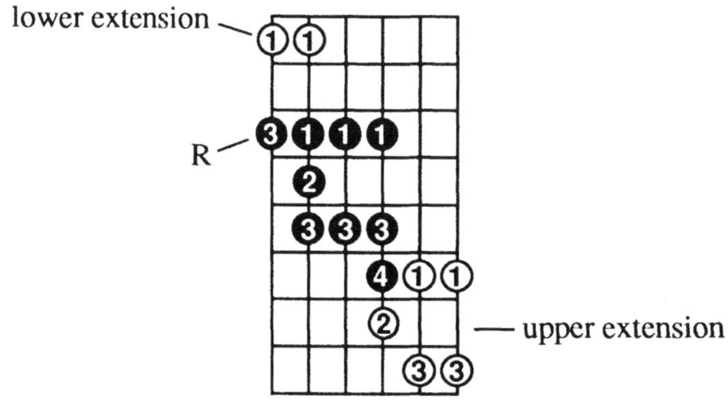

Written below are the notes and tablature for the A blues scale with the lower and upper extensions. Because it is the blues scale for the key of ***A***, the scale is positioned with the root on the sixth string, fifth fret.

62

The next solo is in the key of A and uses the blues scale with the upper and lower extensions.

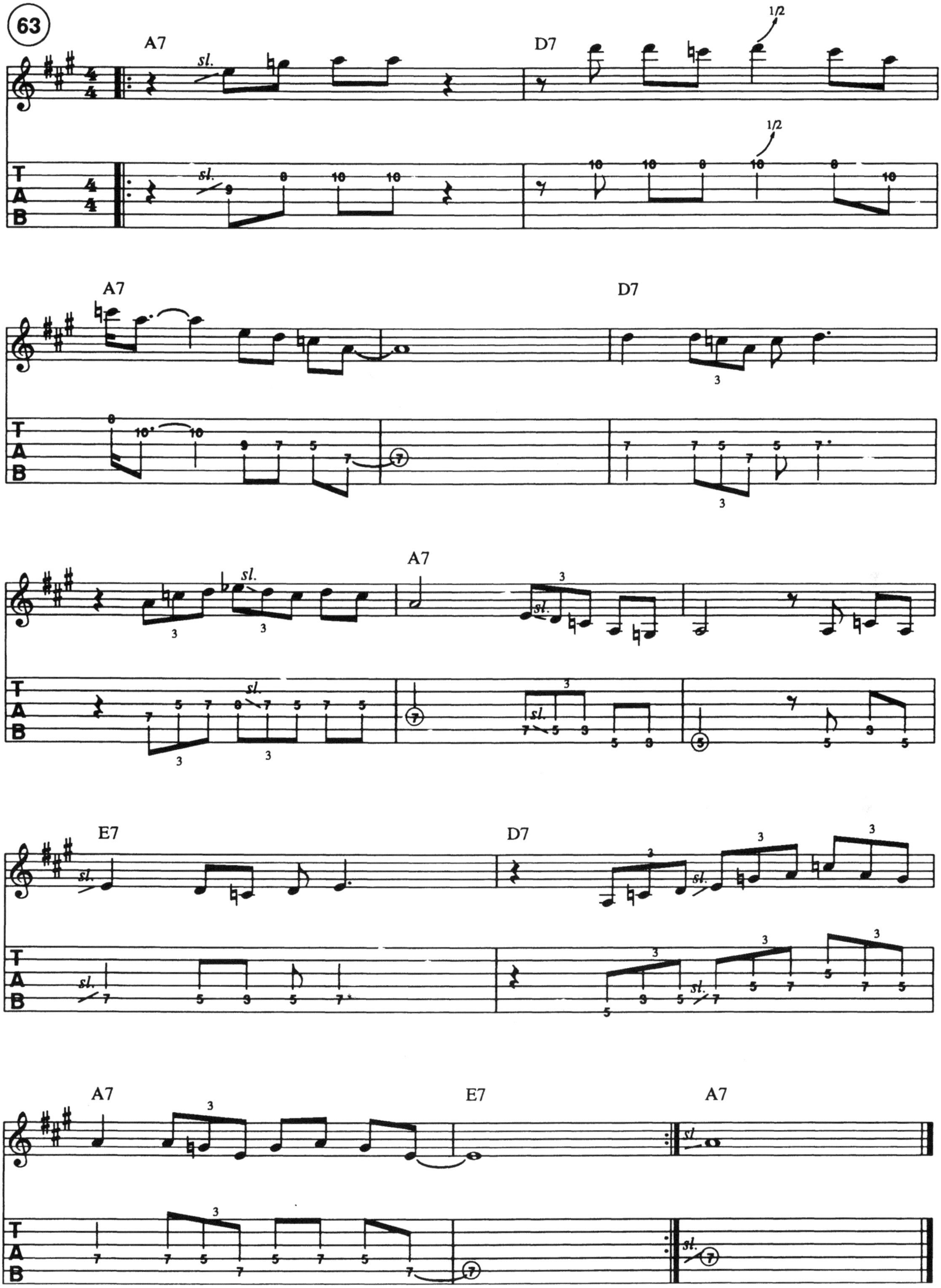
63
A7
D7
A7
D7
A7
E7
D7
A7
E7
A7

This next solo is in the key of A minor. It also uses the A blues scale with the upper and lower extensions. Notice the solo is in 12/8 time. If you're unsure about the time values of the notes, refer to the "Time Values" section at the beginning of this book.

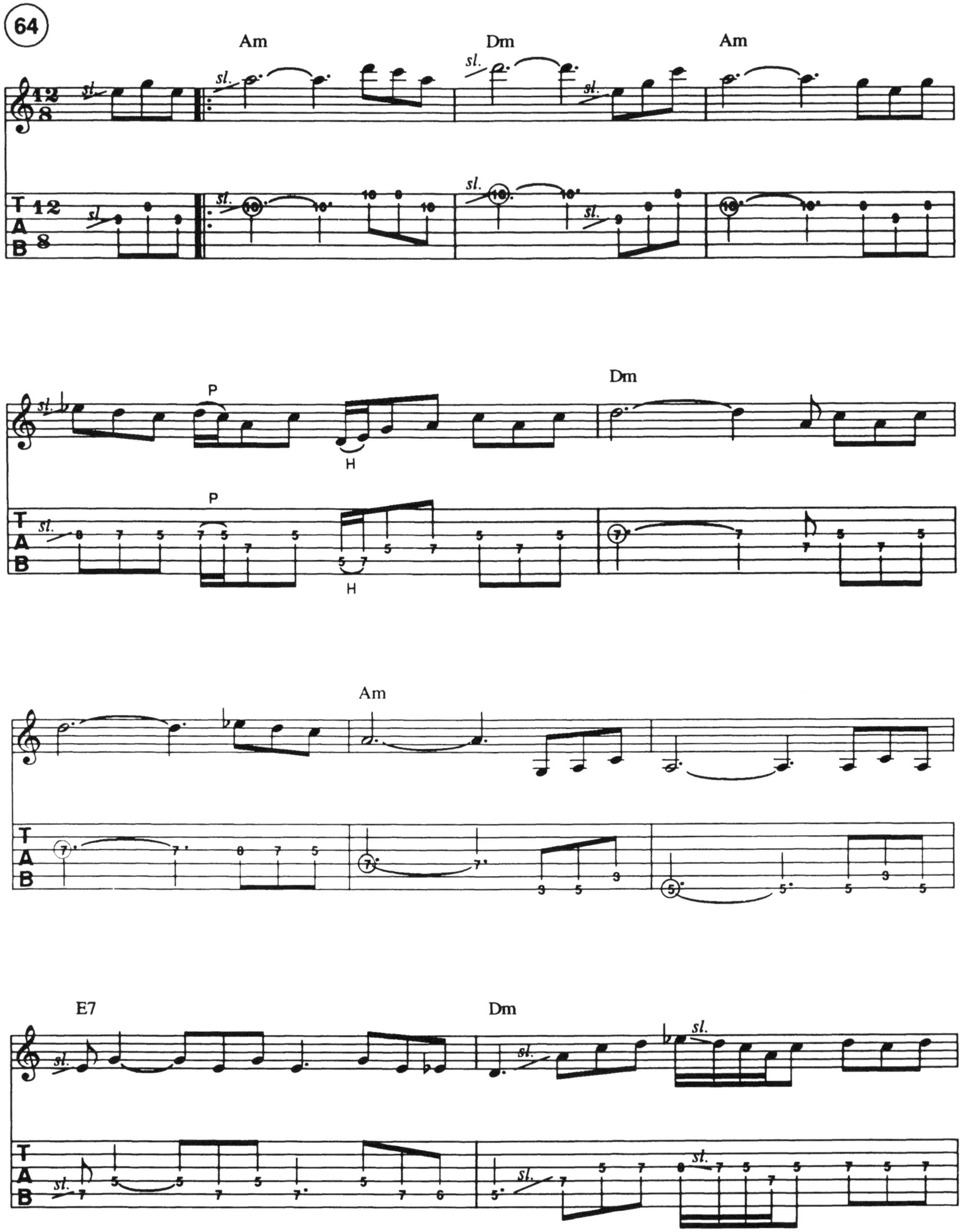

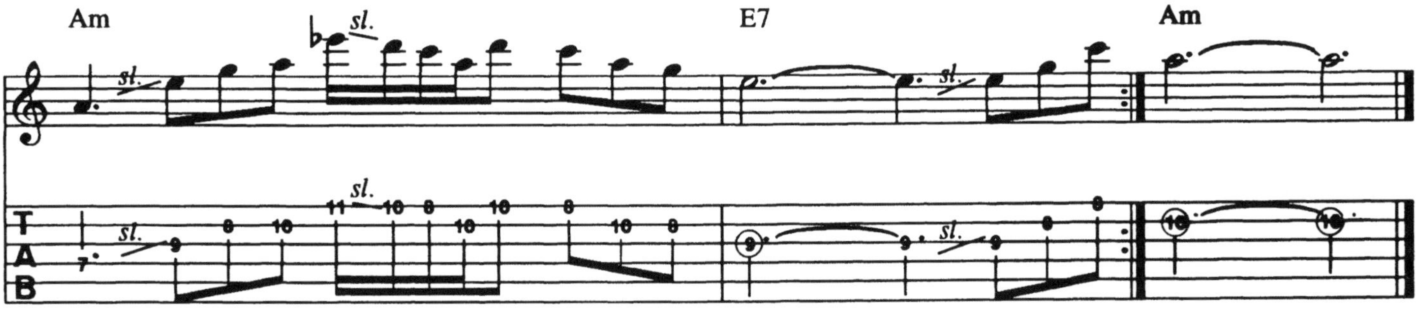

The following diagram shows the blues scale with the root on the fifth string. Like the blues scale with the root on the sixth string, this scale pattern can be positioned anywhere on the neck. The letter name of the note with the "R" pointing to it will be the letter name of the scale. The empty circles indicate to play the string open. When the pattern is moved up the neck, these notes are played with the left-hand first finger.

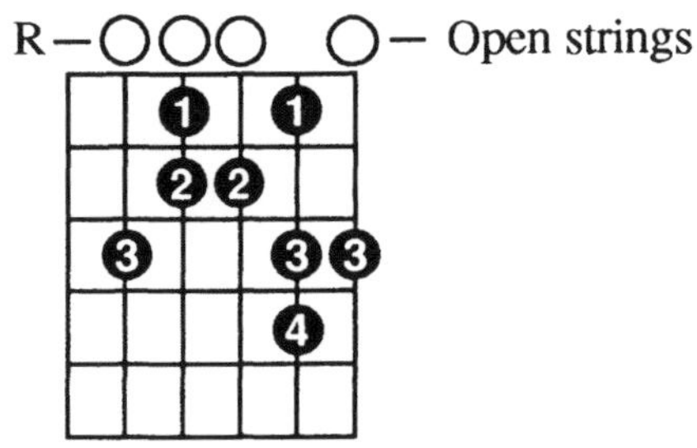

The chart below gives the fret numbers and names of the notes for locating the roots on the fifth string.

Fret	0	1	2	3	4	5	6	7	8	9	10	11	12
Root Name	A	A♯ B♭	B	C	C♯ D♭	D	D♯ E♭	E	F	F♯ G♭	G	G♯ A♭	A

The notes in the A blues scale, with the root on the fifth string, are written below. To play the blues scale for the key of A, the pattern should be positioned so the root is on the fifth string, open.

65

Play the following solos (in A minor) which use the A blues scale with the root on the fifth string open.

67

Jimmy's Shuffle

Because the following progression is a blues in the key of C, the C blues scale is used for the solo. The blues scale with the root on the fifth string is the scale which has been used. The scale pattern is positioned so the root is on the fifth string, third fret. Remember, even though the chords change, you can play the scale which has the same letter name as the first chord through the entire progression.

68

The next diagram shows the upper extension of the blues scale with the root on the fifth string. Written below the diagram are the notes and tablature for the C blues scale with the upper extension. Because it is the *C* blues scale, the root has been positioned on the fifth string, third fret.

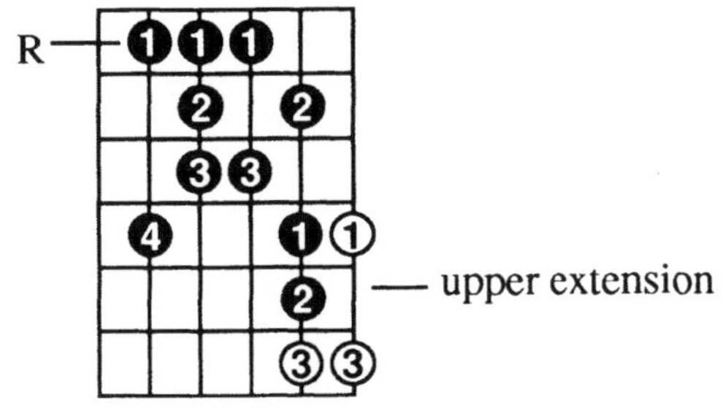

69

The following solo uses the upper extension of the C blues scale with the root on the fifth string, third fret.

70

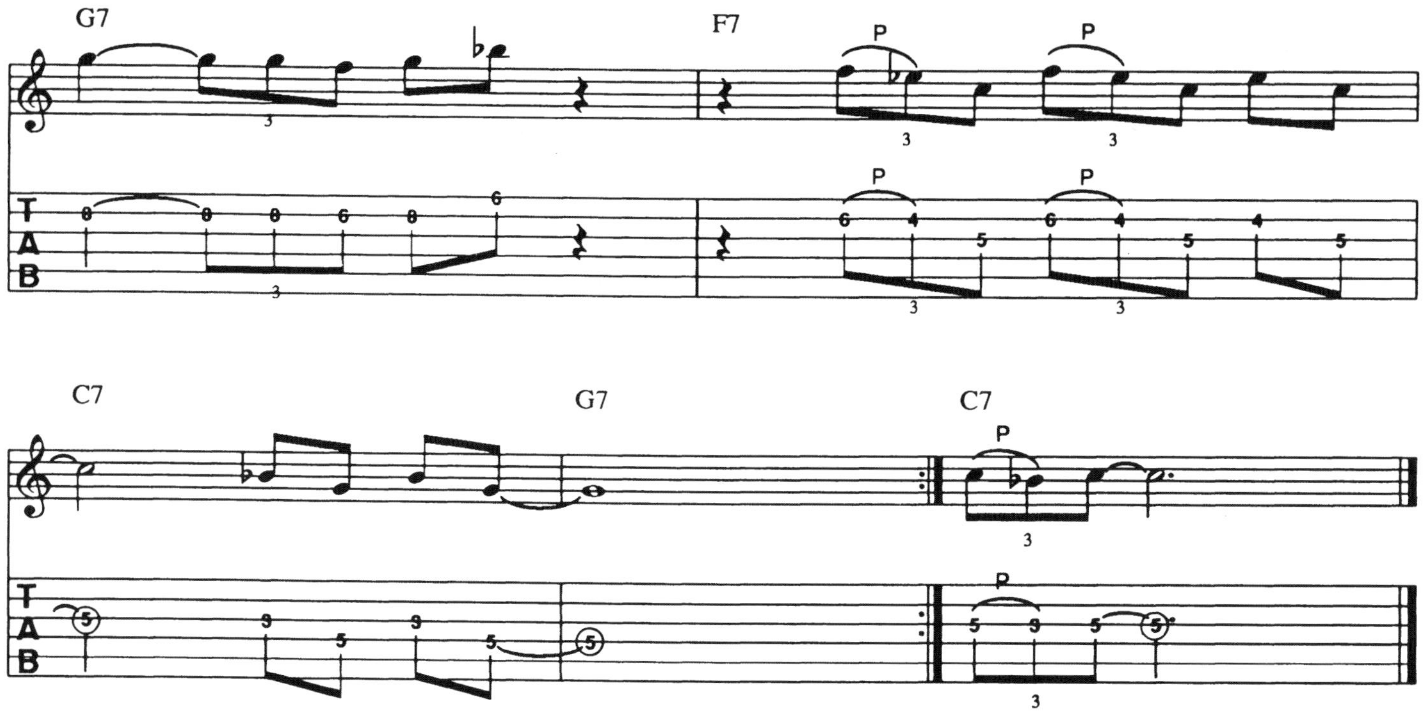

The following diagram shows the lower extension of the blues scale with the root on the fifth string.

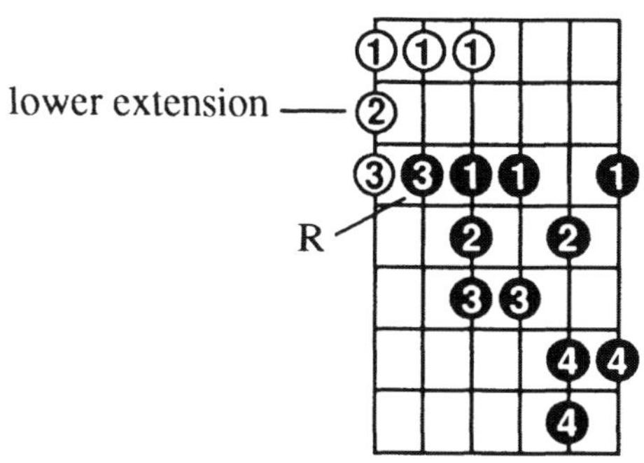

Written below are the notes and tablature for the C blues scale with the lower extension. Because it is the *C* blues scale, the root has been positioned on the fifth string, third fret.

71

The next solo uses the lower extension of the C blues scale with the root on the fifth string, third fret.

72

The next diagram shows the lower and upper extensions of the blues scale with the root on the fifth string.

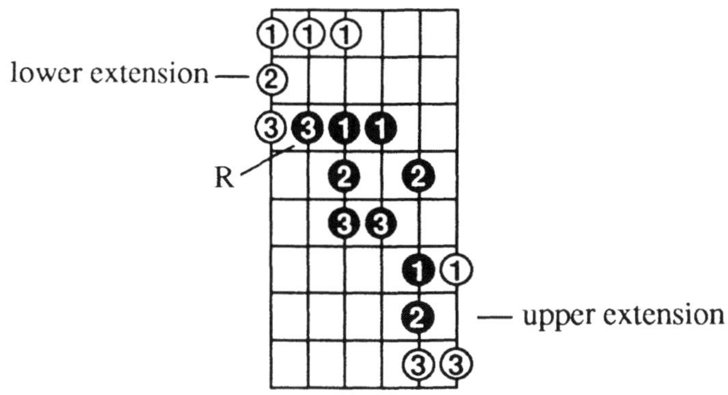

Written below are the notes and tablature for the *C* blues scale with the lower and upper extensions. The root of this scale is on the fifth string, third fret (C).

73

The following solo uses the lower and upper extensions of the C blues scale which has its root on the fifth string, third fret.

74

The following diagram shows how the blues scales with their roots on the sixth and fifth strings (and their extensions) can connect. This makes it possible to cover the entire neck regardless of the key in which you are playing. The empty circles are the blues scale with the root on the sixth string, and the solid dots are the blues scale with the root on the fifth string. Practice creating your own improvised solos by connecting the scales. Remember to position the scales so the root has the same letter name as the key in which you are playing.

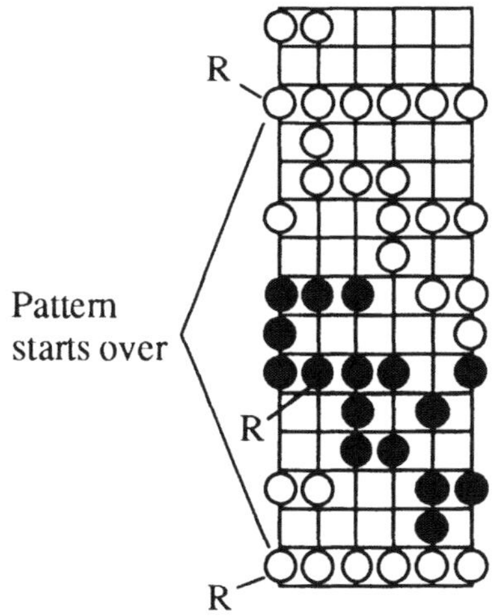

VIII
Double Stops

The term "double stop" means two strings are played at one time. When using the pick, be sure to play the two strings quickly so they sound at the same time. The following diagram shows the possible double stops for the key of E. The lines connecting the circles show which notes can be played together. Below the diagram, the double stops for the key of E are written in standard notation and tablature. Like barre chords and the blues scale, the double stops can be moved to work for any key by placing the note with the "R" pointing to it on the desired key.

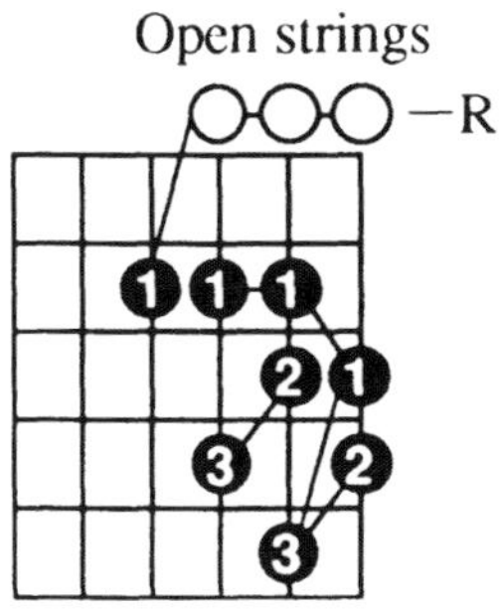

75

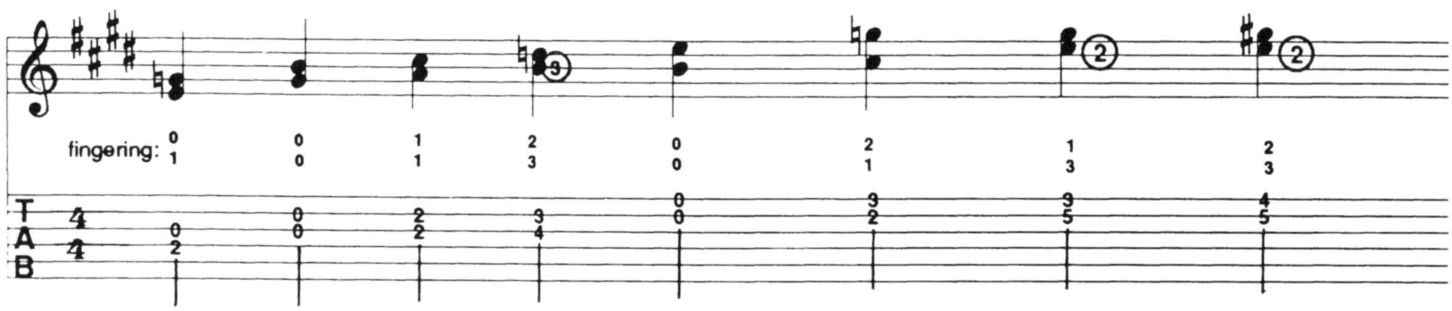

Practice the next two solos which contain double stops for the key of E. Use a pick to play these solos.

76

Double Stop Blues

77

E7
B7
A7
E7
B7
B7
E7
A7
E7
B7
fermata (hold)
A7
E7
B7
E7
strum

IX
Fingerpicking Solos

This section of the book contains fingerpicking blues solos. These solos are written in three different styles: those which have a steady bass, those which have an alternating bass, and those which have a boogie woogie (or boogie) bass. In these fingerpicking styles, the right thumb plays the bass notes (strings 6, 5, and 4), and the right-hand fingers play the melody (usually on strings 1, 2, and 3).

In a "steady-bass" style, the thumb plays the same bass note (which has the same name as the chord for that measure) on each beat of the measure. The fingers play at the same time, or between the thumb strokes. This style of soloing was commonly used by early blues guitarists.

The following exercise will help prepare you to play the solos which have a steady bass. In all of the solos in this section of the book, the notes (or numbers) written with the stems going down are to be played with the thumb. The notes (or numbers) written with the stems going up are to be played with the fingers (generally, the first and second fingers of the right hand). The choice of which finger to use is up to you. Do not use the little finger. If you do not know the meaning of a notation, refer to the "Definitions" section at the beginning of this book.

All of the notes in the following exercise are played with the right-hand thumb.

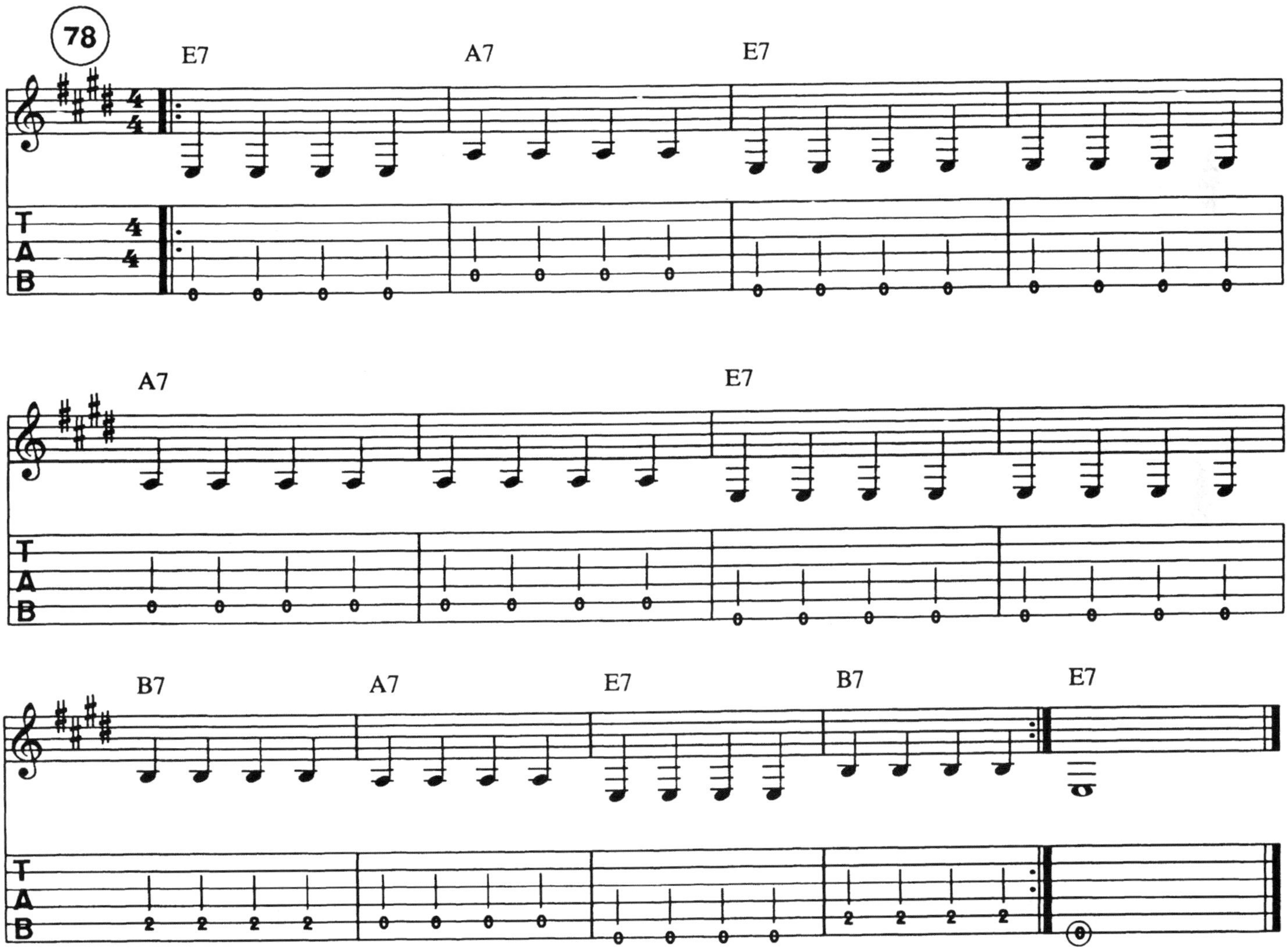

Unless otherwise indicated, all of the fingerpicking solos in this section of the book should be played using the shuffle (or swing) rhythm (♫ = ♪♪ triplet) rather than even eighth notes.

Practice the next few solos in which the thumb plays a steady bass. Remember, the notes with the stems going down are to be played with the thumb, and the notes with the stems going up are to be played with the fingers.

79
E7
A7
E7
B7
A7
E7
B7
E7
B7
E7

80
E7
A7
E7
B7
A7
E7
T
A
B

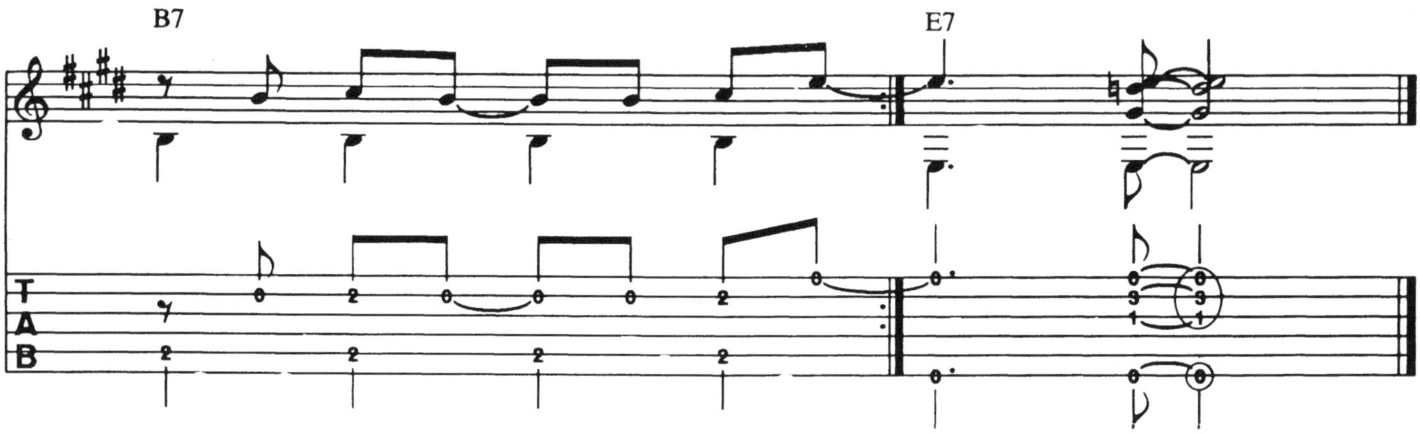

Bob's Blues

The next exercise shows what the thumb plays in the steady-bass style solos in the key of A. Play all of the notes in this exercise with the right-hand thumb.

82

Practice the following steady-bass style solos in the key of A.

84
A7
D7
A7
D7
A7
E7
sl.
P
H

D7
A7
E7
A7
A7
85
A7
D7
A7
D7
sl.
sl.

A7
E7
D7
A7
B♭7 A7
sl.
P

In another type of fingerpicking solo, the thumb alternates between two strings while the fingers play the melody. This is sometimes referred to as the "alternating-bass" style. This technique is commonly used in playing ragtime solos.

The next exercise will get your thumb used to alternating between two strings. It is common in this style to hold the chord which is written above the measure. If a note that you are going to play is not in the chord, modify the fingering of the chord to enable you to get that note. Try to hold as much of the chord as possible.

86

The next exercise shows how the right-hand fingers play between the thumb strokes. This creates an interesting pattern which could be used as an accompaniment for blues songs. Try using this "fingerpicking pattern" to accompany some of the songs in the key of E which are found earlier in this book.

A note which has the stem going down and up is to be played with the right-hand thumb. It is connected rhythmically to the next note.

"Oscar's Blues" is a fingerpicking solo which uses the alternating-bass technique. Remember, while playing the notes in each measure, try to hold the chord written above the measure. The chord may have to be modified slightly by lifting off a finger, or adding a finger, to play the written notes. Hold as much of the chord as possible.

Oscar's Blues

Another technique used in fingerpicking solos is to have the thumb play a boogie woogie bass line while the fingers play the melody or chords.

The next exercise shows the boogie bass line which would be played by the thumb. Do not hold the chords while playing this exercise. Try to use the left-hand fingering which is written in the standard notation.

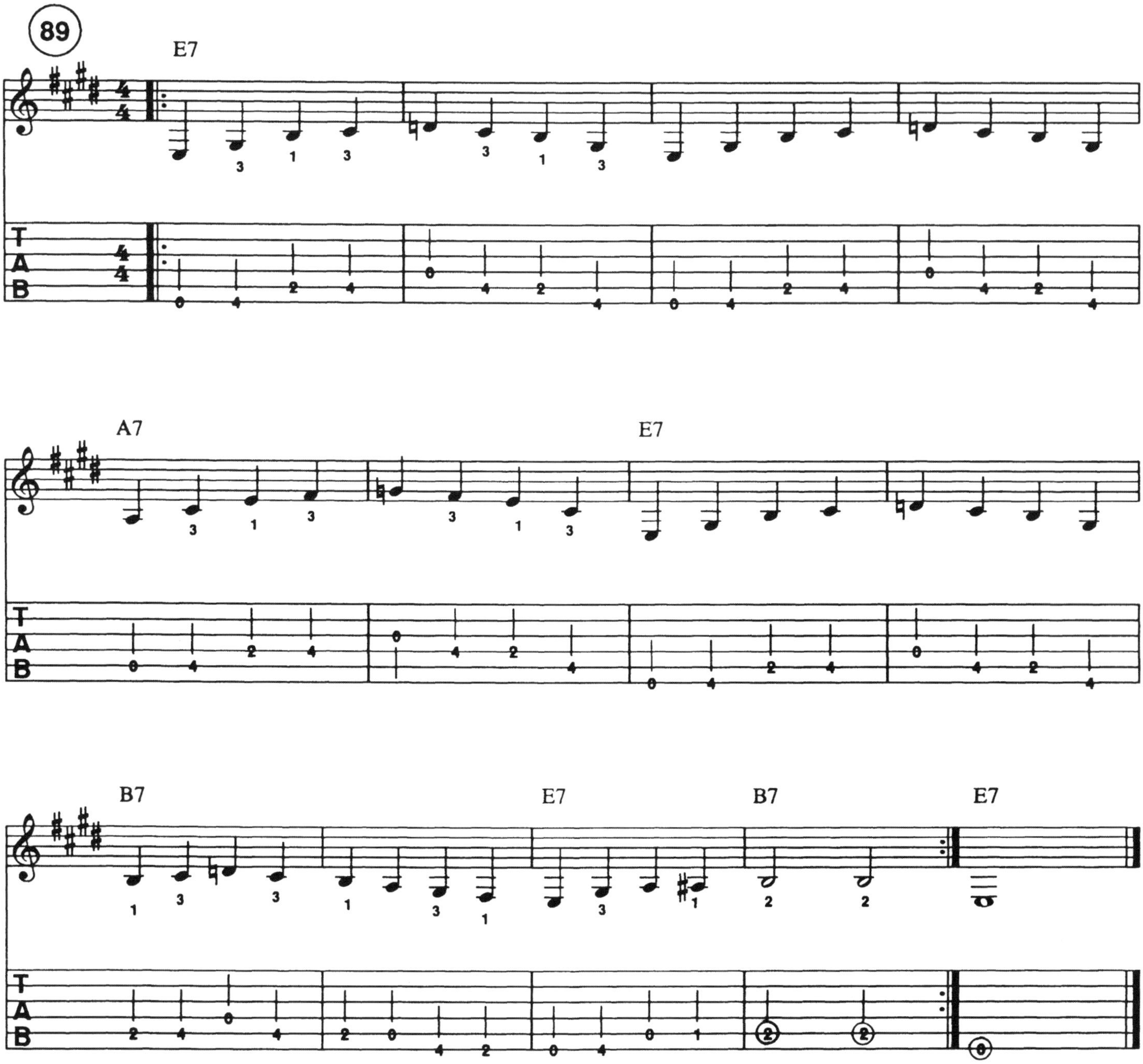

The next fingerpicking solo has the thumb playing a boogie bass line and the first two fingers of the right hand playing between the thumb strokes.

Create your own fingerpicking solos using the steady-bass, alternating-bass, and boogie-bass techniques. Use the notes of the blues scale for your melodies.

Good luck and keep practicing!